PRENTICE HALL WRITER'S SOLUTION

Grammar Practice Book

DIAMOND

PRENTICE HALL
Upper Saddle River, New Jersey
Needham, Massachusetts

Copyright © 1998 by Prentice-Hall, Inc., a Viacom Company, Upper Saddle River, New Jersey 07458. All rights reserved. Student worksheets may be duplicated for classroom use, the number not to exceed the number of students in each class. Notice of copyright must appear on all copies. No other part of this book may be reproduced or transmitted in any form or by any means, electronic or mechanical, including photocopying, recording, or by any information storage or retrieval system, without permission in writing from the publisher. Printed in the United States of America.

ISBN 0-13-434645-9

2 3 4 5 6 7 8 9 10   01 00 99

Contents

I Grammar

1 The Parts of Speech 5
- 1.1 Nouns and Pronouns 5
- 1.2 Verbs 7
- 1.3 Adjectives and Adverbs 10
- 1.4 Prepositions, Conjunctions, and Interjections 12
- 1.5 Reviewing Parts of Speech 15

2 Basic Sentence Parts and Patterns 16
- 2.1 Subjects and Verbs 16
- 2.2 Subjects in Different Kinds of Sentences 18
- 2.3 Complements 20
- 2.4 Basic Sentence Patterns 22
- 2.5 Diagraming Basic Sentence Parts 24

3 Phrases and Clauses 28
- 3.1 Prepositional Phrases and Appositives 28
- 3.2 Verbals and Verbal Phrases 29
- 3.3 Clauses 31
- 3.4 Sentences Classified by Structure 34
- 3.5 Diagraming Phrases and Clauses 35

4 Avoiding Sentence Errors 43
- 4.1 Fragments and Run-ons 43
- 4.2 Misplaced and Dangling Modifiers 45
- 4.3 Faulty Parallelism 46
- 4.4 Faulty Coordination 47

II Usage

5 Levels of Usage 48
- 5.1 The Varieties of English 48
- 5.2 The History of English 49

6 Verb Usage 50
- 6.1 Verb Tenses 50
- 6.2 The Correct Use of Tenses 53
- 6.3 The Subjunctive Mood 55
- 6.4 Voice 56

7 Pronoun Usage 57
- 7.1 Case 57
- 7.2 Special Problems with Pronouns 60

8 Agreement 61
- 8.1 Subject and Verb Agreement 61
- 8.2 Pronoun and Antecedent Agreement 66
- 8.3 Special Problems with Pronoun Agreement 66

9 Adjective and Adverb Usage 68
- 9.1 Degrees of Comparison 68
- 9.2 Clear Comparisons 70

10 Miscellaneous Problems in Usage 73
- 10.1 Negative Sentences 73
- 10.2 One Hundred Common Usage Problems 75

III Mechanics

11 Capitalization and Abbreviation 76
- 11.1 Capitalization 76
- 11.2 Abbreviation 78

12 Punctuation 81
- 12.1 End Marks 81
- 12.2 Commas 82
- 12.3 Semicolons and Colons 85
- 12.4 Quotation Marks and Underlining 86
- 12.5 Dashes, Parentheses, and Brackets 89
- 12.6 Hyphens and Apostrophes 91

IV Composition—The Writer's Techniques

13 The Writing Process 93
- 13.1 Prewriting 93
- 13.2 Writing 95
- 13.3 Revising 96
- 13.4 Finding Your Own Appraoch 97

14 The Use of Words 99
- 14.1 Using Words Effectively 99
- 14.2 Using Words in Special Ways 102

15 Sentence Style 103
- 15.1 Improving Your Sentences 103
- 15.2 Creating Special Effects 106

16 Clear Thinking in Writing 108
- 16.1 Connecting Ideas Clearly 108
- 16.2 Avoiding Problems in Logic 111

V Composition—Forms and Process of Writing

17 Paragraphs 113
- 17.1 Understanding Paragraphs 113
- 17.2 Writing a Paragraph 116

18 Kinds of Writing 117
- 18.1 Expository and Persuasive Writing 117
- 18.2 Descriptive and Narrative Writing 119

19 Essays 121
- 19.1 Understanding Essays 121
- 19.2 Writing an Essay 122
- 19.3 Writing an Expository Essay 123
- 19.3 Writing a Persuasive Essay 124
- 19.3 Writing an Informal Essay 135

20 Research Papers 126
- 20.1 Understanding Research Papers 126
- 20.2 Writing a Research Paper 127

21 Writing About Literature 128
- 21.1 Book Reports 128
- 21.1 Writing a Book Report 129
- 21.2 Literary Analyses 130
- 21.2 Writing a Literary Analysis 131

22 Personal Writing 132
- 22.1 Journals 132
- 22.2 Writing an Anecdote 133
- 22.2 Writing a First-Person Narrative 134
- 22.2 Writing an Autobiography 135

23 Short Stories 136
- 23.1 Understanding Short Stories 136
- 23.1 Writing a Story 138

24 Letters and Applications 139
- 24.1 Personal Letters 139
- 24.2 Business Letters 140
- 24.3 Applications 141

25 Essay Exams and Précis 142
- 25.1 Essay Exams 142
- 25.2 Précis 144

VI Vocabulary and Spelling

26 Vocabulary Building 145
- 26.1 Techniques for Building Vocabulary 145
- 26.2 Using Context 147
- 26.3 Using Structure 148
- 26.4 Exploring Etymologies 150

27 Spelling Improvement 151
- 27.1 Techniques for Improving Spelling 151
- 27.2 A Catalog of Spelling Rules 153

VII Study and Research Skills

28 Basic Study Skills 157
- 28.1 Evaluating Your Study Habits 157
- 28.2 Methods of Taking Notes 158

29 Critical-Thinking Skills 159
- 29.1 Forms of Reasoning 159
- 29.2 Language and Thinking 160

30 Reading and Test-Taking Skills 161
- 30.1 Reading Skills 161
- 30.2 Standardized Tests 163

31 Library and Reference Skills 166
- 31.1 Library Skills 166
- 31.2 Reference Skills 167
- 31.3 Dictionary Skills 168

32 Getting a Job 169
- 32.1 Getting a Job 169
- 32.2 Next Steps 170

VIII Speaking and Listening

33 Speaking and Listening Skills 171
- 33.1 Interviews 171
- 33.2 Group Discussions and Parliamentary Procedure 172
- 33.3 Public Speaking 174
- 33.4 Public Debate 175

1.1 Nouns and Pronouns

Nouns

A noun is the name of a person, place, or thing. Singular nouns name one person, place, or thing. Plural nouns name more than one. A concrete noun names something you can see, touch, taste, hear, or smell. An abstract noun names something you can not perceive through your senses. A common noun names any one of a class of people, places, or things. A proper noun names a specific person, place, or thing.

TYPES OF NOUNS		
Singular Nouns	mouse	dish
Plural Nouns	mice	dishes
Concrete Nouns	tomato	bicycle
Abstract Nouns	existence	quality
Common Nouns	day	river
Proper Nouns	Monday	Mississippi River

A collective noun names groups of people or things. A compound noun is composed of two or more words acting as a single unit. Compound nouns may appear in three forms: as separate words, as hyphenated words, or as combined words.

Collective Nouns	Compound Nouns
faculty	office manager
jury	editor-in-chief
team	postmaster

EXERCISE A: Recognizing Nouns. Underline each noun in the sentences below.

EXAMPLE: My <u>parents</u> took a <u>trip</u> to <u>Vienna</u>.

1. Elections arouse strong feelings in many people.
2. The roof of our barn was damaged in the hurricane.
3. Dubrovnik, a resort in Yugoslavia, is on the Adriatic.
4. My friends were delighted by our success in the long jump.
5. Fortunately, it is a short walk to the library.
6. The committee was impressed by our persistence and determination.
7. The orchestra includes strings, woodwinds, and brass.
8. In the morning the director outlined his plan.
9. Amy offered a good explanation for her failure.
10. Mrs. Hope offered Tom a cruise to the West Indies as a reward.

EXERCISE B: Recognizing Collective and Compound Nouns. Write *collective* or *compound* next to each noun.

EXAMPLE: sightseeing   *compound*

1. roommate _____
2. class _____
3. dog tag _____
4. typewriter _____
5. committee _____
6. orchestra _____
7. herd _____
8. sister-in-law _____
9. overboard _____
10. highlight _____

Copyright © by Prentice-Hall, Inc.

1.1 Nouns and Pronouns

Pronouns

A pronoun is a word used to take the place of a noun. The noun it substitutes for is called an antecedent.

PRONOUNS AND ANTECEDENTS
ANTECEDENT   PRONOUN   PRONOUN
Priscilla asked *her* brother if *she* could borrow a sweater.

Study the types of pronouns in the chart and note their uses.

TYPES OF PRONOUNS		
Type	**Use**	**Examples**
Personal	Refer to particular people, places, or things	I, he, she, it, we, you, they
Indefinite	Refer to people, places, or things without specifying which ones	each, everyone, some, both
Interrogative	Used to ask questions	what, which, who, whom, whose
Demonstrative	Used to point out a particular person, place, or thing	this, that, these, those

EXERCISE A: Recognizing Pronouns and Antecedents. Underline the personal pronoun in each sentence and circle its antecedent.

EXAMPLE: (Bob) lent Sally <u>his</u> typewriter.

1. Will Ruth bring her stereo to the party?
2. Because of his injury, Ted was unable to play.
3. The doctor said that he would begin first with eye examinations.
4. Jeff, will you please mow the lawn now.
5. With her team about to lose, Betty scored the winning basket.
6. Maimonides completed his first major work in 1168.
7. In the accident the bus lost its rear axle.
8. Allison asked Ted if she could go.
9. When they completed the project, the students went to lunch.
10. How will you feel later, Lee Ann?

EXERCISE B: Recognizing Different Types of Pronouns. Underline the pronoun in each sentence and tell whether it is *personal, indefinite, interrogative,* or *demonstrative*.

EXAMPLE: <u>Everyone</u> should vote in the election.   *indefinite*

1. This is much too expensive. _____
2. We have decided to visit Spain next year. _____
3. Whom did Kim ask for directions? _____
4. Has the coach spoken to both of the boys? _____
5. Someone just rang the bell. _____

NAME _____ CLASS _____ DATE _____

1.2 Verbs

Action Verbs and Linking Verbs

An action verb tells what action someone or something is performing. A linking verb connects its subject with another word that renames or describes the subject.

Action Verbs	Linking Verbs
For years the people *waited*.	Picasso *was* a famous painter.
Our visitors *left* after lunch.	This stew *tastes* delicious.

EXERCISE A: Identifying Action and Linking Verbs. Underline each verb. Write *action* or *linking* after it.

EXAMPLE: The river <u>swells</u> near the cove. _____action_____

1. Mary Grace seems unusually poised. _____
2. In the morning the freighter sailed. _____
3. In 1066 William the Conqueror landed in England. _____
4. Trenton is the capital of New Jersey. _____
5. In a short time my sister grew tall. _____
6. After a year, Stan became our captain. _____
7. The magician reached into the velvet bag. _____
8. Unfortunately, the speaker was late. _____
9. My grandfather looks older these days. _____
10. Unnoticed, we slipped out the door. _____

EXERCISE B: Using Linking Verbs. From the list below, choose an appropriate linking verb to use in each of the following sentences.

    sound   look   smell   taste   be
    grow   turn   feel   become   appear

EXAMPLE: The music ___sounds___ delightful.

1. The train _____ to be late today.
2. Susan _____ our new president.
3. I _____ a better typist quickly.
4. The rhubarb pie _____ too sour.
5. Grandmother doesn't _____ well today.
6. Your new scent _____ fantastic.
7. Sweet cream, unless refrigerated, _____ bad rapidly.
8. Before the game, the team _____ unhappy.
9. In those shoes, he _____ taller.
10. On the phone my father _____ discouraged.

NAME _____ CLASS _____ DATE _____

1.2 Verbs

Transitive and Intransitive Verbs

A verb is transitive if it directs action toward someone or something named in the same sentence. A verb is intransitive if it does *not* direct action toward someone or something named in the same sentence.

Transitive	Intransitive
Steve *built* a bookcase.	Jeanne *rowed* across the lake.
Paula *brought* Lucy home.	Grandma *slept* restfully.

EXERCISE A: Identifying Transitive and Intransitive Verbs. Label each underlined verb as transitive or intransitive.

EXAMPLE: Jennie wiped her windshield carefully. *transitive*

1. We plant an assortment of vegetables every spring. _____
2. The Great Mosque of Samarra has existed since 847. _____
3. Several pages of the document were on file. _____
4. We told the class about the book fair. _____
5. The soloist played Vivaldi's *Mandolin Concerto*. _____
6. Three major religions consider Jerusalem a holy city. _____
7. Smiling, the heroine disappeared into the shadows. _____
8. My aunt always keeps a rescue ladder in her bedroom. _____
9. Mother still talks about President Kennedy. _____
10. All morning the strange rumble grew louder. _____

EXERCISE B: Writing Sentences with Transitive and Intransitive Verbs. Complete the sentences below. For sentences with transitive verbs, add a noun or pronoun toward which the verb directs its action.

EXAMPLE: Transitive: Judy quickly opened the *letter.*
            Intransitive: The victim smiled *bravely.*

1. Intransitive: The principal agreed _____
2. Transitive: Later, she reached _____
3. Transitive: Suddenly, the passengers saw a _____
4. Intransitive: The bus screeched _____
5. Transitive: The mayor told the _____
6. Intransitive: At dawn the rooster crowed _____
7. Intransitive: The team traveled _____
8. Transitive: Dr. Greer gave the _____
9. Intransitive: The astronaut spoke _____
10. Transitive: Take the _____

NAME _____ CLASS _____ DATE _____

1.2 Verbs

Verb Phrases

A verb that is made up of more than one word is a verb phrase. A verb phrase is formed by adding helping verbs to another verb in a sentence.

VERB PHRASES
The president *will appoint* a committee.
We *could have reached* another decision.
Better prepared, she *might have been chosen* to play a leading role.
I *have* certainly *admired* your work.
She *will* hopefully not *reject* the post.

EXERCISE A: Identifying Verb Phrases. Underline all parts of the verb phrase in each sentence. Do not underline words that interrupt a verb phrase.

EXAMPLE: I <u>had</u> almost <u>forgotten</u> about the meeting.

1. We should have taken a less congested route.
2. My parents will definitely not give us permission to go.
3. Throughout the Roman period, Ostia had been a leading naval port.
4. Have they opened their presents yet?
5. We could not have gotten a better break in the game.
6. All the stars will appear at the spring festival.
7. By the age of ten she had almost grown to full height.
8. *The Marriage of Figaro* has been performed twice this season.
9. Undoubtedly, she could not be selected to run.
10. The judges have already made their decision.

EXERCISE B: Using Verb Phrases. Complete each of the following sentences with an appropriate verb phrase that includes the verb in parentheses.

EXAMPLE: _____ you _____ the new position yet? (accept)
     <u>Have</u> you <u>accepted</u> the new position yet?

1. _____ you _____ _____ to the prom? (invite)
2. The office _____ _____ on the second floor. (locate)
3. She _____ already _____ her prize. (receive)
4. Annette _____ _____ _____ _____ at the news. (surprise)
5. Tomorrow, they _____ _____ to Chicago. (fly)
6. We _____ definitely _____ to remain. (agree)
7. The roof _____ _____ this morning. (repair)
8. They _____ _____ _____ to Cape Cod for years. (go)
9. _____ you _____ the shirts and the pants? (buy)
10. The doctor _____ not _____ you a new prescription. (give)

NAME _____ CLASS _____ DATE _____

1.3 Adjectives and Adverbs

Adjectives

An adjective is a word used to describe a noun or pronoun or to give a noun or pronoun a more specific meaning. Like nouns, adjectives can be compound—that is, they can be made up of more than one word—or proper. Proper adjectives are formed from proper nouns and always begin with a capital letter. A pronoun is used as an adjective if it modifies a noun. The chart below summarizes the kinds of pronouns used as adjectives and their use.

Possessive Adjectives		Demonstrative Adjectives	Interrogative Adjectives	Indefinite Adjectives		
				Singular	Plural	Either
my	its	this	which	another	both	all most
your	our	that	what	each	few	any other
his	their	these	whose	either	many	more some
her		those		neither	several	

EXERCISE A: Adding Pronouns Used as Adjectives. Fill in each blank with the kind of adjective given in parentheses.

EXAMPLE: I know _those_ people sitting in the corner. (demonstrative)

1. _____ students were still taking the test. (indefinite)
2. _____ question do you want me to answer? (interrogative)
3. Is this _____ coat or yours? (possessive)
4. There are _____ books I want to read. (indefinite)
5. Jill and Vincent brought _____ new puppy to my house. (possessive)
6. _____ term paper is due next week. (possessive)
7. _____ hat is on the table? (interrogative)
8. This article is more interesting than _____ one. (demonstrative)
9. May I have _____ piece of pie? (indefinite)
10. Are _____ records yours or mine? (demonstrative)

EXERCISE B: Using Proper Adjectives in Sentences. In the space provided, write a sentence using each word below as an adjective.

EXAMPLE: Parisian   _Mrs. Townson wore a Parisian gown._

1. French _____
2. Alaskan _____
3. Latin American _____
4. Himalayan _____
5. Spanish _____
6. Canadian _____
7. Roman _____
8. Elizabethan _____
9. European _____
10. Emersonian _____

NAME _____ CLASS _____ DATE _____

1.3 Adjectives and Adverbs

Adverbs

An adverb is a word that modifies a verb, an adjective, or another adverb.

Adverbs Modifying Verbs	
Where? The tuxedos will be delivered *here*.	**When?** According to the plans, our cousins will arrive *tomorrow*.
In what manner? She speaks *rapidly*.	**To what extent?** Diane *nearly* won.
Adverbs Modifying Adjectives	**Adverbs Modifying Adverbs**
To what extent? He is *too* curious.	**To what extent?** She skates *very* well.

EXERCISE A: Recognizing Adverbs and the Words They Modify. Underline the adverb in each sentence. In the space provided, tell whether it modifies a verb, an adjective, or another adverb. Some sentences have two adverbs.

EXAMPLE: My brother drives <u>recklessly</u>.   *verb*

1. Are your friends still angry? _____
2. The destructive flood stopped there. _____
3. My mother paints really well. _____
4. I think the package was delivered yesterday. _____
5. The shortstop fielded every ball gracefully. _____
6. She has already written to her senator. _____
7. I always organize material carefully. _____
8. The speaker is obviously late. _____
9. She talks incessantly about her boyfriend. _____
10. Your little sister seems very polite. _____

EXERCISE B: Adding Adverbs to Sentences. Fill in the blanks below with appropriate adverbs.

EXAMPLE: Everyone in my family spells   *poorly* .

1. Our college applications arrived _____.
2. They have _____ returned our phone calls.
3. The road _____ changed from three lanes into one.
4. Madeline is _____ finished with her research paper.
5. This digital watch is _____ reliable.
6. Put the new bookcase _____.
7. She has _____ taken sides against me.
8. Speak _____ when you address the student government.
9. With time short, she shopped _____.
10. I can _____ understand her reasoning.

1.4 Prepositions, Conjunctions, and Interjections

Prepositions

A preposition is a word that relates a noun or pronoun that appears with it to another word in the sentence.

FREQUENTLY USED PREPOSITIONS			
about	between	in	over
across	by	into	to
at	before	near	through
among	for	of	under
below	from	on	with

A prepositional phrase begins with a preposition and ends with a noun or pronoun called the object of the preposition.

PREPOSITIONAL PHRASE	
Prepositions	**Objects of Prepositions**
with	my *friends*
between	*us*
next to	the old *building*

EXERCISE A: Identifying Prepositions. Underline each preposition in the sentences below. Some sentences have more than one.

EXAMPLE: In the morning they traveled to the city.

1. She asked for passes to the football game.
2. This agreement is strictly between you and me.
3. They arrived from Spain about ten in the evening.
4. Over the hill is a gas station with a rest room.
5. We spoke for hours about our class reunion.
6. The price of this stereo is below our regular discount price.
7. Go through the corridor into the other building.
8. With great joy we walked across the stage.
9. I received a special award from the coach.
10. Your hat is under the mirror near the umbrella.

EXERCISE B: Identifying Prepositional Phrases. In each sentence place parentheses around each prepositional phrase. Some sentences have more than one.

EXAMPLE: (At dawn) we drove (to the agricultural fair).

1. The room in the attic is filled with old furniture.
2. The card shop is not far from the park.
3. The cave paintings at Lascaux were discovered in 1940.
4. Near the hotel you will find a group of craft shops.
5. There are no secrets between Sally and me.
6. I walked through the town in an hour and a half.
7. For years the author waited for a letter from her son.
8. A group of travelers arrived by air.
9. In high school I studied the flute with Mr. Poole.
10. They drove through the night to the next town.

1.4 Prepositions, Conjunctions, and Interjections

Conjunctions

A conjunction is a word used to connect other words or groups of words. Coordinating conjunctions and correlative conjunctions join similar kinds of words or groups of words that are grammatically alike. Subordinating conjunctions connect subordinate clauses with independent clauses in complex sentences.

COORDINATING CONJUNCTIONS						
and	but	for	nor	or	so	yet

CORRELATIVE CONJUNCTIONS		
both . . . and	either . . . or	neither . . . nor
whether . . . or	not only . . . but also	

FREQUENTLY USED SUBORDINATING CONJUNCTIONS				
after	as soon as	even though	than	when
although	as though	if	though	whenever
as	because	since	unless	wherever
as if	before	so that	until	while

EXERCISE A: Identifying Conjunctions. Underline the conjunction in each sentence. Write a *C* if it is coordinating, *CR* if it is correlative, or *S* if it is subordinating.

EXAMPLE: <u>Either</u> I will go, <u>or</u> I will send my sister.   *CR*

1. Bob arrived late even though he caught the first flight. _____
2. I wanted to play in the homecoming game, but I hurt my knee. _____
3. Not only is he a scholar, but he is also a fine athlete. _____
4. Mother said she would write or phone from Bermuda. _____
5. Hebron and Beersheba were cities in ancient Judah. _____
6. Whether he wins or loses is not really important. _____
7. As soon as the hurricane ended, we began to rescue people. _____
8. Both Whitney and Tiffany agreed to volunteer. _____
9. We visited the science museum while they waited. _____
10. Neither my teacher nor my father liked my idea. _____

EXERCISE B: Using Coordinating, Correlative, and Subordinating Conjunctions in Sentences. Complete each sentence. Make sure each subordinating conjunction is followed by a full clause.

EXAMPLE: If _____, I will write you.
          If *you send me your address*, I will write you.

1. Either I _____, or I _____.
2. Since _____, I bought a new stereo.
3. Because _____, she _____.
4. Both _____ and _____ phoned yesterday.
5. We hoped to win, but _____.

1.4 Prepositions, Conjunctions, and Interjections

Interjections

An interjection is a word that expresses strong feeling or emotion. Interjections have no grammatical connection to the sentences in which they appear.

A LIST OF COMMON INTERJECTIONS				
ah	dear	hey	ouch	well
aha	goodness	hurray	psst	whew
alas	gracious	oh	tsk	wow

Interjections are punctuated with either a comma or an exclamation mark. The exclamation mark (!) is used to express strong emotion.

EXERCISE A: Identifying Interjections. Underline the interjection in each sentence below.

EXAMPLE: "Gracious," said Grandmother, "what will happen next?"

1. "Ouch," said the batter, after fouling a ball off his foot.
2. "Alas! It is almost midnight," cried Cinderella.
3. Well, I think we have only two possible options.
4. I reminded Billy to stop saying "wow" all the time.
5. "Psst," said the stranger. "How do you get to the station?"
6. I haven't heard anyone say "tsk!" for a while.
7. "Hurray!" we shouted. "We have finally won a game."
8. Father confessed, "Oh, I'm afraid we're lost."
9. Whew! Am I glad I've finished my research paper.
10. My aunt often begins her sentences with "gracious."

EXERCISE B: Writing Sentences with Interjections. Write an original sentence using each interjection below.

EXAMPLE: Dear, _____.
         Dear, _I wonder why they are late._

1. "Hurray," said our manager, "_____."
2. Wow! _____
3. "Ouch!" she cried. "_____."
4. Hey! Wait a minute. _____
5. My uncle said, "Tsk! _____."
6. Well, _____
7. Mary exclaimed, "Gee, _____."
8. Aha, now _____
9. "Tarnation," said Gramps, "_____."
10. It's all over. Alas, _____

NAME _____ CLASS _____ DATE _____

1.5 Reviewing Parts of Speech

Words as Different Parts of Speech

The way a word is used in a sentence determines what part of speech it is.

DIFFERENT USES OF A WORD
As a noun: The campers built a small *fire*.
As a verb: Managers may *fire* poor workers.
As an adjective: Slaughterhouse-Five describes a *fire* storm in Dresden.

EXERCISE A: Identifying Parts of Speech. On each blank at the right, write the part of speech of each underlined word.

EXAMPLE: <u>Before</u> breakfast, I brushed my teeth. ___preposition___
<u>Before</u> she came, she phoned. ___conjunction___

1. My older brother always drives too <u>fast</u>. _____
2. She lost three pounds during her <u>fast</u>. _____
3. Trucks are not allowed to use the <u>fast</u> lane. _____
4. Show the <u>group</u> your new cassette deck. _____
5. Our agency only handles <u>group</u> sales. _____
6. Before beginning, <u>group</u> all the ingredients together. _____
7. <u>Since</u> this morning, she hasn't felt well. _____
8. <u>Since</u> I bought the car, I have had nothing but trouble. _____
9. The <u>inside</u> of the jewel box is velvet. _____
10. The <u>inside</u> lane is much faster. _____

EXERCISE B: Using Words as Different Parts of Speech. Construct sentences of your own using the following words as indicated.

EXAMPLE: Use *storm* as a noun. ___A sudden storm struck.___
Use *storm* as a verb. ___"Storm the trenches," the major cried.___

1. Use *light* as an adjective. _____
2. Use *light* as a verb. _____
3. Use *file* as an adjective. _____
4. Use *file* as a verb. _____
5. Use *file* as a noun. _____
6. Use *after* as a preposition. _____
7. Use *after* as a conjunction. _____
8. Use *low* as an adjective. _____
9. Use *low* as an adverb. _____
10. Use *storm* as an adjective. _____

NAME _____ CLASS _____ DATE _____

2.1 Subjects and Verbs

Complete Subjects and Complete Predicates

A sentence is a group of words with two main parts: a complete subject and a complete predicate. Together, these parts express a complete thought.

Complete Subjects	Complete Predicates
The weary travelers	staggered into the mining camp.
Business in our society	is based on making a profit.

Fragments

A fragment is a group of words that does not express a complete thought.

Fragments	Complete Sentences
A person with diabetes.	A person with diabetes should avoid using sugar.
Offered us directions to the mall.	The toll taker at the bridge offered us directions to the mall.
In the middle of the film.	In the middle of the film the projector broke.

EXERCISE A: Recognizing Complete Subjects and Predicates. Draw a vertical line between each complete subject and predicate.

EXAMPLE: Montgomery Center in Vermont | is close to Canada.

1. Waffles and ice cream is a longtime favorite of mine.
2. The parishioners reacted enthusiastically to our appeal.
3. Carrying their gear, the campers departed.
4. The Board of Inquiry reached a unanimous decision.
5. Beethoven's *Creatures of Prometheus* has been recorded many times.
6. My mother uses a recipe for oatmeal cookies passed down through generations.
7. My trip to Madrid and Barcelona has been postponed.
8. The governor, a tall, impressive man, entered the auditorium.
9. Several different flights to Dallas are now available.
10. This Thanksgiving will be a most joyous holiday.

EXERCISE B: Distinguishing Between Sentences and Fragments. In the blanks below, write *S* for each sentence and *F* for each fragment.

EXAMPLE: Bad weather canceled the flight. __*S*__

1. The map of the United States. ____
2. Attempted to contact the principal several times. ____
3. At the end of the hearing. ____
4. A salesman telephoned this morning. ____
5. Jeanne's explanation was absurd. ____
6. Troubled by inconsistencies in his testimony. ____
7. In spite of every attempt to help the students. ____
8. Strangely, the baby only crawls backwards. ____
9. An angry inspector from the health department. ____
10. Agreed to postpone the decision. ____

NAME _____ CLASS _____ DATE _____

2.1 Subjects and Verbs

Simple Subjects and Simple Predicates

The simple subject is the essential noun, pronoun, or group of words acting as a noun that cannot be left out of the complete subject. The simple predicate is the essential verb or verb phrase that cannot be left out of the complete predicate. In the chart below each simple subject is underlined once, each simple predicate twice.

SIMPLE SUBJECTS AND SIMPLE PREDICATES	
Complete Subjects	**Complete Predicates**
An important <u>announcement</u>	<u><u>interrupted</u></u> the TV program.
The <u>road</u> to Boston	<u><u>has been flooded</u></u> by the heavy rains.

EXERCISE A: Recognizing Simple Subjects and Predicates. Underline the simple subjects once and the simple predicates twice in the sentences below.

EXAMPLE: The reckless <u>athlete</u> <u><u>endangered</u></u> his teammates.

1. A box of deluxe chocolates makes an excellent gift.
2. The manila envelope had obviously been opened by someone.
3. At sixteen Beethoven traveled to Vienna to meet Mozart.
4. *Raiders of the Lost Ark* should become a movie classic.
5. The stamps in Grandfather's collection are extremely valuable.
6. Groups of travelers were stranded by the snowstorm.
7. At the prom Betty met her old boyfriend.
8. The house on the hill contains a secret passageway.
9. An increasing number of complaints have recently been received.
10. A telltale smudge on the document aroused suspicions.

EXERCISE B: Using Simple Subjects and Predicates to Write Sentences. Use each simple subject and simple predicate below to write a complete sentence. Draw a vertical line between the complete subject and the complete predicate.

EXAMPLE: rules are _____Some rules | are hard to enforce._____

1. principal announced _____
2. train halted _____
3. report indicated _____
4. recipe uses _____
5. uncle trembled _____
6. package has arrived _____
7. team agreed _____
8. state senator wrote _____
9. grandmother pickled _____
10. swimmer will attempt _____

NAME _____ CLASS _____ DATE _____

2.2 Subjects in Different Kinds of Sentences

The Four Functions of Sentences

The four sentence types are *declarative*, *interrogative*, *imperative*, and *exclamatory*. A declarative sentence states an idea and ends with a period. An interrogative sentence asks a question and ends with a question mark. An imperative sentence gives an order or direction and ends with a period or exclamation mark. An exclamatory sentence conveys strong emotion and ends with an exclamation mark.

FOUR FUNCTIONS OF SENTENCES
Declarative: Toronto is not far from Buffalo. *Interrogative:* Which composer wrote the famous *The Four Seasons*? *Imperative:* Renew your driver's license this week. *Exclamatory:* What an amazing custom!

EXERCISE A: Identifying the Four Functions of Sentences. Write *D* for a declarative sentence, *Int.* for an interrogative sentence, *Imp.* for an imperative sentence, and *E* for an exclamatory sentence. Add the proper punctuation mark at the end of each sentence.

EXAMPLE: The Normans invaded England in 1066. __D__

1. Who knows where the shoulder pads are _____
2. Every good cake recipe contains sugar _____
3. Take all the groceries into the kitchen _____
4. What a truly unpleasant situation this is _____
5. The Turks captured Constantinople in 1453 _____
6. How many new members must we recruit this month _____
7. Make certain that you research your paper carefully _____
8. What a horrible turn of events _____
9. Which reference book do you recommend _____
10. The lecture will be preceded by a short film _____

EXERCISE B: Writing Original Sentences. Complete the work below.

1. Write two declarative sentences. _____
   _____
   _____

2. Write three interrogative sentences. _____
   _____
   _____
   _____

3. Write three imperative sentences. _____
   _____
   _____
   _____

4. Write two exclamatory sentences. _____
   _____
   _____

2.2 Subjects in Different Kinds of Sentences

Hard-to-Find Subjects

In most sentences the subject comes before the verb. This arrangement is called *normal word order*. In some sentences, however, the verb comes first, and the word order is *inverted*. If there is a problem finding a subject, change the sentence back to normal word order, placing the subject first.

HARD-TO-FIND SUBJECTS	
Problem Sentences	**In Normal Word Order**
Near the road is a *telephone*.	A *telephone* is near the road.
There is a *salesman* at the door.	A *salesman* is at the door.
Here are your *notes*.	Your *notes* are here.
What did *you* want?	*You* did want what.
Write your congresswoman.	(*You*) write your congresswoman.

EXERCISE A: Finding Hard-to-Find Subjects. Draw a single line under each subject and a double line under each verb.

EXAMPLE: There <u><u>are</u></u> several <u>answers</u> to that question.

1. Here is a bushel of apples.
2. Where is the title of your story?
3. What did you buy at the clothing sale?
4. About two miles down the road is a modern hotel.
5. There have been a number of strange reactions to her speech.
6. Between the hospital and the garage is a fast-food restaurant.
7. Tell us in your own words about the accident.
8. There are two interesting routes to Halifax.
9. When has the operation been scheduled?
10. In the back of the drawer are several pens.

EXERCISE B: Changing Sentences to Normal Word Order. Each sentence below is in inverted word order. Rewrite the sentence, changing it to normal word order. Place a single line under the subject and a double line under the verb.

EXAMPLE: Here are your books.
        <u>Your books</u> <u><u>are</u></u> here.

1. Near the window is a box of tissues.

2. Here are the keys to the safe.

3. Have you chosen a secretary?

4. There are three strange men at the door.

5. What did Pat think of his explanation?

2.3 Complements

Direct Objects

A *complement* is a word or group of words that completes the meaning of the predicate of a sentence. One of the most common complements, the direct object, is a noun, pronoun, or group of words acting as a noun that receives the action of a transitive verb.

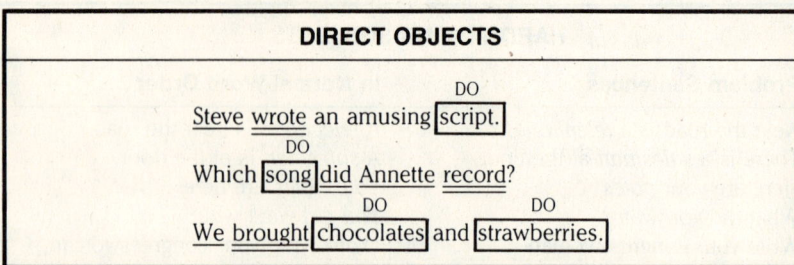

Indirect Objects

An indirect object is a noun or pronoun that appears with a direct object and names the person or thing that something is given to or done for.

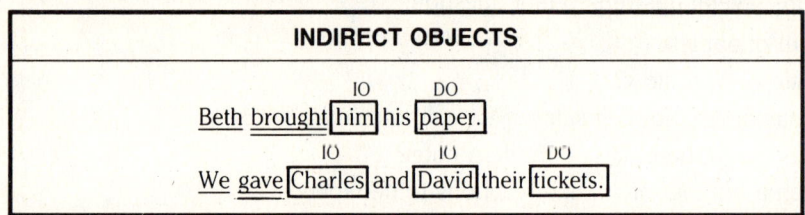

Indirect objects often appear with these transitive verbs: *ask, bring, buy, give, lend, make, promise, show, teach, tell,* or *write*.

EXERCISE A: Identifying Direct Objects. Draw a box around each direct object in the sentences below.

EXAMPLE: The Senate passed an important bill.

1. Stew the vegetables in a little beef broth.
2. Jason needs a dictionary and a thesaurus.
3. Which exit do you take from the parkway?
4. I will ask him about the interview.
5. Every morning Father always buys a newspaper.
6. She drinks either tea or coffee.
7. The artist painted a subdued sunset.
8. Can you describe the hotel to us?
9. I will recommend him and her for the two positions.
10. Melody prepared an outstanding graphic for the fair.

EXERCISE B: Finding Indirect Objects. Draw a box around each indirect object in the sentences below. Also underline each direct object.

EXAMPLE: I wrote the governor a letter.

1. My sister showed the class her award.
2. For his birthday we promised Dad a new stereo.
3. Will you give them the bad news?
4. I will teach Susan a new computer language.
5. Why don't you lend Judy and him your old typewriter?

2.3 Complements

Objective Complements

An objective complement is an adjective, noun, or group of words acting as a noun that follows a direct object and describes or renames it.

OBJECTIVE COMPLEMENTS
DO   OC Most <u>observers</u> <u>thought</u> the decision incorrect. DO   OC The <u>committee</u> <u>appointed</u> Bill chairperson.

Subject Complements

A subject complement is a noun, pronoun, or adjective that follows a linking verb and tells something about the subject of the sentence. There are two kinds of subject complements: predicate nominatives and predicate adjectives. A predicate nominative is a noun or pronoun that renames or identifies the subject. A predicate adjective is an adjective that describes the subject.

SUBJECT COMPLEMENTS
PN *Predicate Nominative:*   Helen <u>was</u> our <u>coach</u>.   PA *Predicate Adjective:*   Your <u>pudding</u> <u>is</u> delicious.

EXERCISE A: Recognizing Objective Complements. Underline the objective complement in each sentence below. Then write whether it is a noun or an adjective.

EXAMPLE: Our team thinks the coach <u>unreasonable</u>. _____*adjective*_____

1. In this particular case we will keep the files open. _____
2. The class made Michelle president. _____
3. The inspector thought the plan dangerous. _____
4. The court appointed him executor of the estate. _____
5. After Bob's accident, the coach named Paul captain. _____
6. The college registrar considers her ineligible. _____
7. My sister painted her apartment brown. _____
8. Will our team name Maria spokesperson? _____
9. Most of us found the opera uninteresting. _____
10. The family thought the present inappropriate. _____

EXERCISE B: Recognizing Predicate Nominatives and Predicate Adjectives. Underline the predicate nominatives and predicate adjectives. Next to each sentence write either *PN* (predicate nominative) or *PA* (predicate adjective).

EXAMPLE: His father is unusually <u>intelligent</u>. _____*PA*_____

1. Our counselor often seems distracted. _____
2. Through his own efforts he had become our captain. _____
3. Her chief interest has always been her job. _____
4. The architect's plan for the new theater is impressive. _____
5. Grandmother's old ring must be very valuable. _____

2.4 Basic Sentence Patterns

Five Basic Patterns with Complements

In the English language, subjects, verbs, and complements follow five basic sentence patterns.

SENTENCE PATTERNS WITH TRANSITIVE VERBS	
Patterns	**Examples**
S-AV-DO	I often visit [Philadelphia]. (DO)
S-AV-IO-DO	Father bought [us] (IO) a new [computer] (DO).
S-AV-DO-OC	The school considers the [pamphlet] (DO) [dangerous] (OC).
SENTENCE PATTERNS WITH LINKING VERBS	
S-LV-PN	Leonore is a [cheerleader] (PN).
S-LV-PA	The country road was [bumpy] (PA).

EXERCISE A: Recognizing the Parts of Basic Sentence Patterns. Underline each subject once and each verb twice. Draw a box around each complement.

EXAMPLE: In the morning we had a quick [breakfast].

1. Paula told the principal the truth about the accident.
2. The entire exhibit was unusually effective.
3. After much deliberation they reached a final decision.
4. Parts of the bicycle are rusty.
5. We brought our cousins a box of chocolate chip cookies.
6. I consider his plan premature.
7. Uncle Morris is a craftsman with a fine reputation.
8. After the meeting Gloria felt uncertain.
9. Dorothy was a woman with considerable talent.
10. He colored the entire graphic blue.

EXERCISE B: Recognizing Basic Sentence Patterns. Write the pattern of each sentence in Exercise A.

EXAMPLE: _S-AV-DO_

1. _____
2. _____
3. _____
4. _____
5. _____
6. _____
7. _____
8. _____
9. _____
10. _____

NAME _____ CLASS _____ DATE _____

2.4 Basic Sentence Patterns

Inverted Patterns

In an inverted sentence pattern, the subject is never first.

PATTERNS IN INVERTED QUESTIONS	
Patterns	**Examples**
HV-S-V-COMP	Did the Yankees win their [game]? (DO)
COMP-HV-S-V	Which [teams] do you follow? (DO)
COMP-HV-S-V-COMP	Which [card] did Mary give her [sister]? (DO, IO)
PATTERNS IN SENTENCES BEGINNING WITH *THERE* OR *HERE*	
V-S	Here is my car.
PATTERNS INVERTED FOR EMPHASIS	
COMP-S-V	What high [hopes] I had! (DO)
COMP-S-V-COMP	What [trouble] he caused [us]! (DO, IO)

EXERCISE A: Recognizing the Parts of Sentences with Inverted Patterns. In the sentences below, underline each subject once, underline each verb twice, and draw a box around each complement.

EXAMPLE: There is my friend.

1. Which girl did you ask to the dance?
2. Here comes Leroy.
3. What a great time they had!
4. What a good friend she is!
5. Did Mary pass her math test?
6. Will Rocky come to the party?
7. Which sports do you like?
8. Which road do you take to Vermont?
9. How happy I was!
10. Here is the end.

EXERCISE B: Recognizing Inverted Sentence Patterns. Write the pattern of each sentence in Exercise A.

EXAMPLE: _V-S_

1. _____
2. _____
3. _____
4. _____
5. _____
6. _____
7. _____
8. _____
9. _____
10. _____

2.5 Diagraming Basic Sentence Parts

Subjects, Verbs, and Modifiers

In a sentence diagram, the subject and verb are written on a horizontal line with the subject on the left and the verb on the right. A vertical line separates the subject and verb. Adjectives and adverbs are placed on slanted lines directly below the words they modify.

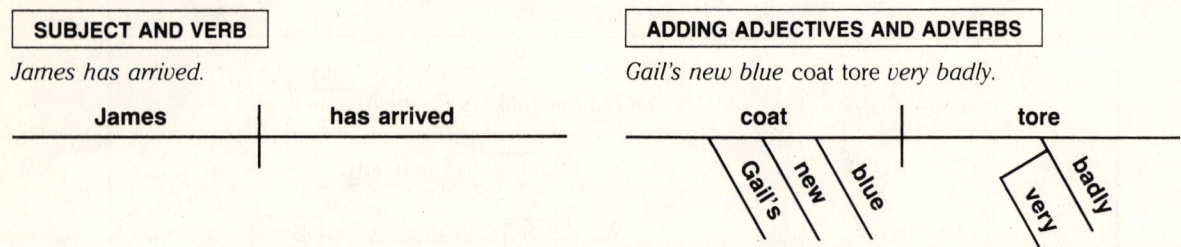

Orders and directions are diagramed with the understood subject *you* in parentheses. *Here* and *there* are usually adverbs and diagramed accordingly. When *there* is an expletive, it is positioned on a short line above the subject. The expletive style is also used for interjections and nouns of direct address.

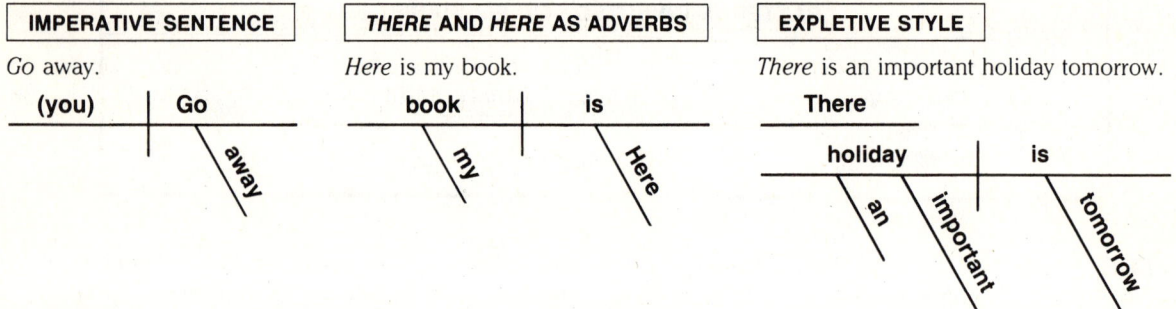

EXERCISE A: Diagraming Subjects, Verbs, and Modifiers. Correctly diagram each sentence in the space provided. Refer to the examples above if you need to.

1. Her mother drives very carefully.

2. My baby brother speaks quite well.

3. Fresh green vegetables are sold here.

EXERCISE B: More Work with Diagrams. Correctly diagram each sentence.

1. Drive carefully.

2. There is a funny movie playing nearby.

2.5 Diagraming Basic Sentence Parts

Adding Conjunctions

Conjunctions are generally shown in a diagram on a dotted line between the words being connected. In sentences with compound subjects and/or verbs, the horizontal line of the diagram is split so each of the compound parts appears on a line of its own. If compound verbs share a helping verb, the helping verb is placed on the main line of the diagram. If each part of the compound verb has its own helping verb, each helping verb is placed on the line with its verb.

COMPOUND SUBJECT AND VERB

My *homework* and my *project are written* and *typed*.

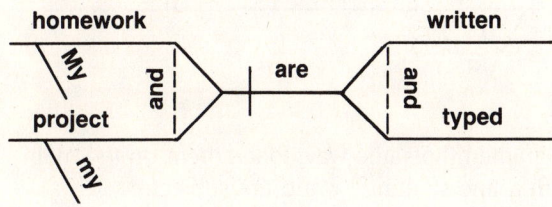

OTHER USES OF CONJUNCTIONS

Blue and *white* floodlights shine *brightly* and *dramatically*.

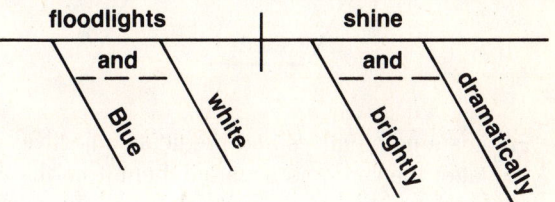

EXERCISE A: Diagraming Sentences with Conjunctions. Correctly diagram each sentence in the space provided.

1. This basketball player jumps well and rebounds effectively.

2. Young and old people participate eagerly and often.

3. The suspects were questioned and released.

EXERCISE B: More Work with Conjunctions. Correctly diagram each sentence.

1. The is shining brightly and intensely.

2. My father and mother are leaving.

2.5 Diagraming Basic Sentence Parts

Complements

Place a direct object on the main horizontal line after the verb; separate it from the verb with a short horizontal line. Place an indirect object under the verb on a short horizontal line extending from a slanted line. An objective complement is placed next to the direct object on the horizontal line and separated from it with a slanted line.

DIRECT AND INDIRECT OBJECTS

Father brought *them* new *bracelets*.

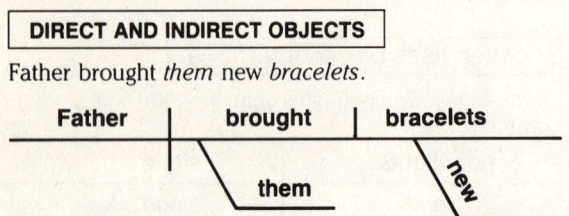

OBJECTIVE COMPLEMENTS

The council appointed *Bill treasurer*.

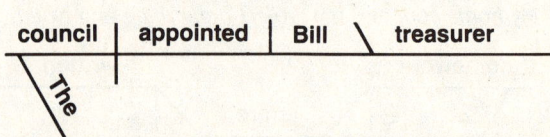

Predicate nominatives and predicate adjectives are diagramed the same way. Place them on the main line after the verb and separate them from the verb with a line slanting toward the subject.

PREDICATE NOMINATIVE

The Olympus is a sophisticated *camera*.

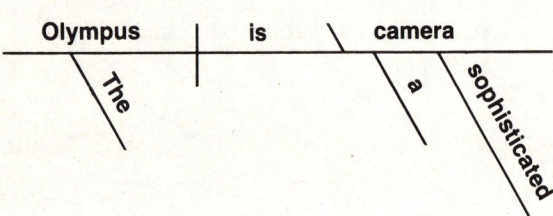

PREDICATE ADJECTIVE

Your new graphic is undoubtedly superb.

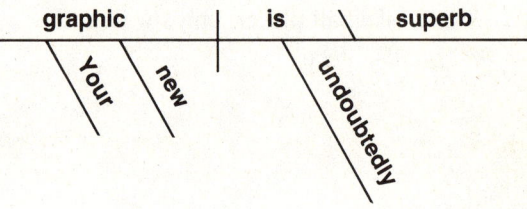

EXERCISE A: Diagraming Sentences with Complements. Correctly diagram each sentence in the space provided.

1. Her spring outfit is unusually attractive.
2. The principal gave Betsy the message.

EXERCISE B: More Work with Complements. Correctly diagram each sentence.

1. My best friend was elected chairperson.
2. She colored the letters gray and gold.

NAME _____ CLASS _____ DATE _____

3.1 Prepositional Phrases and Appositives

Prepositional Phrases

A phrase is a group of words, without a subject and verb, that is used in a sentence as one part of speech. An adjective phrase is a prepositional phrase that modifies a noun or pronoun by telling what kind or which one.

ADJECTIVE PHRASES
The closet *in the den* is empty. (*Which* closet?)
I bought a robe *with pockets*. (*What kind* of robe?)

An adverb phrase is a prepositional phrase that modifies a verb, adjective, or adverb by pointing out where, when, in what manner, or to what extent.

ADVERB PHRASES
The boat disappeared *during a storm*. (Disappeared *when*?)
Sandy and Bob drove *across the country*. (Drove *where*?)
Beth arrived late *for work*. (Late to what extent?)

EXERCISE A: Identifying Adjective and Adverb Phrases. Underline each prepositional phrase in the sentences below. Then circle the word or words each phrase modifies and label the phrase *adjective* or *adverb*.

EXAMPLE: A (seat) on the bus is expensive. ___adjective___

1. The manager is unhappy with Jody's performance. _____
2. After lunch Trish and I visited the library. _____
3. This is an apartment with two full baths. _____
4. A group of traveling actors visited the campus. _____
5. An important conference convened in Ottawa. _____
6. The football coach was angry after the game. _____
7. Ted will give his report on medieval customs. _____
8. Mother is ecstatic about her anniversary present. _____
9. At a later time we will tell you the entire story. _____
10. Where can I catch the bus to Boston? _____

EXERCISE B: Writing Sentences with Adjective and Adverb Phrases. Write phrases to complete the following sentences. Then label each phrase as *adjective* or *adverb*.

EXAMPLE: We spoke politely ___to the detective___ ___adverb___

1. I read *Twelfth Night* _____ . _____
2. I bought her birthday present _____ . _____
3. Unfortunately, Toby was late _____ . _____
4. The library _____ did not have it. _____
5. We had to cancel our trip _____

27

Copyright © by Prentice-Hall, Inc.

3.1 Prepositional Phrases and Appositives

Appositives and Appositive Phrases

An appositive is a noun or pronoun placed next to another noun or pronoun to identify, rename, or explain it.

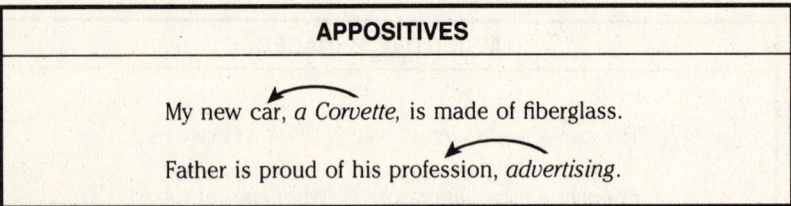

An appositive phrase is a noun or pronoun with modifiers, placed next to a noun or pronoun to add information or details.

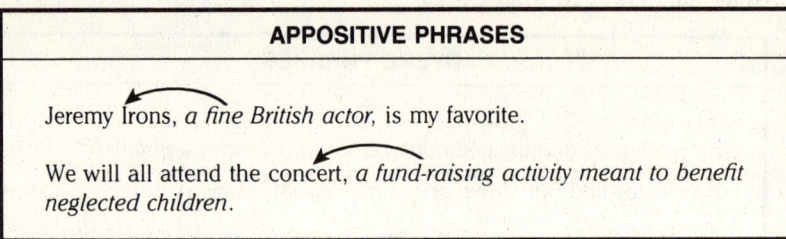

EXERCISE A: Identifying Appositives. Underline the appositive in each sentence. Circle the noun or pronoun it renames.

EXAMPLE: My (brother) William has just been promoted.

1. I read a fascinating book, *Lincoln*, by Gore Vidal.
2. Miss Touvin, a teacher, leads our Service Council.
3. Brad has an unusual hobby, taxidermy.
4. Her new camera, a Hasselblad, is very expensive.
5. The British poet John Donne is still highly regarded.
6. His instrument, the viola, requires great skill.
7. Did you speak to your brother Phil?
8. A British fighter, the Spitfire, probably saved England in the 1940's.
9. Rhonda Evans, a farmer, lives in Vermont.
10. Marty loves playing his favorite instrument, the guitar.

EXERCISE B: Identifying Appositive Phrases. Underline the appositive phrase in each sentence. Circle the noun or pronoun it renames.

EXAMPLE: My favorite (story,) *The Scarlet Ibis* by James Hurst, is available in some anthologies.

1. The Dead Sea Scrolls, ancient writings in Aramaic, stirred many Biblical scholars.
2. His new coat, a garment of cashmere and wool, is quite expensive.
3. I love her special dessert, a dish of berries, bananas, and whipped cream.
4. The graduates, members of the Class of 1975, discussed a reunion.
5. The investigator's files, a record of gambling activities, have been subpoenaed.
6. Lacrosse, a fast-paced, exciting game, is gaining popularity in the United States.
7. I visited my sister's friends, a group of co-eds.
8. You won't believe the first thing you see, a statue of Queen Victoria.
9. The old lamp, a brass hurricane model, is an antique.
10. He has a squalid apartment, two dismal rooms in an attic.

NAME _____ CLASS _____ DATE _____

3.2 Verbals and Verbal Phrases

Participles and Participial Phrases

A verbal is a word derived from a verb but used as a noun, adjective, or adverb. A participle is a verbal that acts as an adjective. A participial phrase is a participle that is modified by an adverb or adverb phrase or that has a complement. The entire phrase acts as an adjective in a sentence. Participles and participial phrases have three forms: present, past, and perfect.

Kinds of Participles	Forms	Examples
Present Participle	Ends in -ing	*Climbing*, she reached the peak.
		A *growing* child needs nourishment.
Past Participle	Usually ends in -ed, sometimes -t, -en, or another irregular ending	The *frightened* man fainted.
		Worried, she consulted a doctor.
Perfect Participle	Includes *having* or *having been* before a past participle	*Having finished*, she handed in her test.
		Having been excused, he left the table.

EXERCISE A: Identifying Present, Past, and Perfect Participles. Underline the participle in each sentence and circle the word it modifies. On the line at the right, write *present*, *past*, or *perfect* to tell which kind it is.

EXAMPLE: Elated, (he) phoned his parents.   *past*

1. Having won, the tennis player accepted the trophy. _____
2. Smiling, my sister accepted her award. _____
3. The old man, hesitating, stumbled across the avenue. _____
4. Relieved, she decided to turn over a new leaf. _____
5. Marie strikes everyone as a dedicated young woman. _____
6. Only a chosen few can participate. _____
7. Irritated, the speaker refused to continue. _____
8. Having been paroled, the ex-convict vowed never to commit another crime. _____
9. The old actress, delighted, took another bow. _____
10. Surprised, he began to stumble over his words. _____

EXERCISE B: Identifying Participial Phrases. Underline each participial phrase and circle the word it modifies.

EXAMPLE: Troubled by her decision, (she) lay awake.

1. Groping in the drawer, she found her passport.
2. The sailor, running at top speed, reached his ship on time.
3. Told to report at once, I knocked on the principal's door.
4. Tired by her journey, she reached the Al-Azhar Mosque in Cairo.
5. The relentless explorer, broken in spirit, decided to turn back.
6. Jogging rapidly, my cousin circled the dam.
7. The figures, computed with amazing speed, proved accurate.
8. The victors, dancing in the streets, soon exhausted themselves.
9. Dismayed at the news, the old man began to cry.
10. The river, swollen to new heights, finally crested.

Copyright © by Prentice-Hall, Inc.

29

3.2 Verbals and Verbal Phrases

Gerunds and Gerund Phrases

A gerund is a verbal that acts as a noun. A gerund phrase is a gerund with modifiers or complements, all acting together as a noun. Gerunds and gerund phrases can be used as subjects, direct objects, indirect objects, objects of prepositions, predicate nominatives, and appositives.

Gerunds	Gerund Phrases
Subject: **Smoking** is no longer allowed here.	*Subject:* **Collecting antiques** is her major interest.
Object of a Preposition: He spoke about **drinking**.	*Object of Preposition:* Mr. Haskis told us about **growing different flowers**.
Predicate Nominative: His great joy is **swimming**.	*Direct Object:* She enjoys **baking fruit pies**.
Appositive: Her obsession, **knitting**, annoys us.	*Indirect Object:* Pam gave **bicycling around the lake** one try only.

Infinitives and Infinitive Phrases

An infinitive is a verbal that generally appears with the word *to* and acts as a noun, adjective, or adverb. An infinitive phrase is an infinitive with modifiers, a complement, or a subject, all acting together as a single part of speech.

Infinitives	Infinitive Phrases
Subject: **To smile** is important when you meet new people	*Subject:* **To practice daily** is not easy for most people.
Direct Object: Our team hopes **to win**.	*Direct Object:* We expect them **to be gone all week**.
Adjective: Here is a book **to read**.	*Adjective:* The way **to reach the hospital** is simple.
Adverb: It is often very hard **to change**.	*Adverb:* They struggled **to remain objective**.

EXERCISE A: Identifying Gerunds and Gerund Phrases. Underline the gerund or gerund phrase in each sentence. In the space provided, tell how it is used.

EXAMPLE: <u>Chewing gum</u> is a bad habit. ____*subject*____

1. I don't recommend driving too fast. _____
2. She was warned about teasing her sister. _____
3. Her lecture gave dreaming a new perspective. _____
4. Traveling is an important part of this job. _____
5. Her fear, growing old, is shared by many. _____

EXERCISE B: Identifying Infinitives and Infinitive Phrases. Underline the infinitive or the infinitive phrase in each sentence. In the space provided, tell whether it is used as a noun, adjective, or adverb.

EXAMPLE: Everyone wants <u>to go swimming</u>. ____*noun*____

1. Jason tries to eat properly every day. _____
2. The museum to visit is not far from here. _____
3. To graduate from college is her first goal. _____
4. Father is about to read to his grandchildren. _____
5. This is an important document to study. _____

3.3 Clauses

Adjective Clauses

A clause is a group of words with its own subject and verb. An independent clause can stand by itself as a complete sentence. A subordinate clause cannot stand by itself as a complete sentence. An adjective is a subordinate clause that modifies a noun or pronoun by telling what kind or which one. Adjective clauses begin with relative pronouns or relative adverbs.

ADJECTIVE CLAUSES

A magazine *which contains similar information* is *Scientific American*.

This is the watch *that Mother wants*.

It is they *who are responsible*.

Relative pronouns act as nouns or adjectives within the adjective clauses. Relative adverbs act as adverbs within the clause. Note that in some sentences, such as the third one below, a relative pronoun may be understood.

THE USES OF RELATIVE PRONOUNS

The clown *who is in the center ring* is the funniest. (subject)

The man *whose coat is torn* looks very unhappy. (adjective)

The skirt *(that) I am wearing* is too long. (understood direct object)

This is the friend of *whom I have spoken*. (object of a preposition)

EXERCISE A: Identifying Adjective Clauses. Underline the adjective clause in each sentence and circle the noun or pronoun it modifies.

EXAMPLE: The (book) which she asked for is too expensive.

1. This is the restaurant which was described in the magazine. _____
2. The story that she told is hardly plausible. _____
3. It is Judy whose invitation was lost. _____
4. Our governor, who has a large private income, travels often. _____
5. Grandfather saves stamps which portray different animals. _____
6. Is this the time that we have waited for? _____
7. A team which doesn't improve should be reorganized. _____
8. Yes, it is I who wrote the appeal to the President. _____
9. The book which she read deals with foreign policy. _____
10. Here are the train tickets that we lost. _____

EXERCISE B: Identifying the Use of Relative Pronouns. Identify the use of each of the relative pronouns in Exercise A as *subject, direct object, object of a preposition,* or *adjective*.

EXAMPLE: The (book) which she asked for is too expensive.   *object of a preposition*

3.3 Clauses

Adverb Clauses

An adverb clause is a subordinate clause that modifies a verb, adjective, adverb, or verbal by telling where, when, in what manner, to what extent, under what condition, or why. Adverb clauses are introduced by subordinate conjunctions such as *although, since, if, when, while, because,* and *where*.

ADVERB CLAUSES	
Modified Word	**Example**
Verb	*When I finish this letter,* I will begin to prepare the budget.
Adjective	I am lost *if I don't read a newspaper every day.*
Adverb	The committee responded faster *than we anticipated.*
Verbal	Laughing *until tears appeared,* Susan stepped into the lobby.

EXERCISE A: Identifying Adverb Clauses. Underline the adverb clause in each sentence and circle the word or words it modifies.

EXAMPLE: I will be (happy) when I have finished this report.

1. The principal was upset after he learned the truth.
2. Sooner than we expected, we received a confirmation of our order.
3. Unless the weather changes rapidly, we will postpone the trip.
4. Smoking where it is prohibited will result in a summons.
5. We can begin the conference since all the participants have arrived.
6. He expects to stay until his mission is completed.
7. Although we played brilliantly, we lost the game.
8. The survey was completed faster than we expected.
9. She is happy if everything goes according to schedule.
10. Eat slowly so that you will digest your food better.

EXERCISE B: Writing Sentences with Adverb Clauses. Add an appropriate adverb clause to each independent clause below.

EXAMPLE: She can't remember ___where she lost the ring___.

1. Faster _____, the flood receded.
2. _____, I will save you a seat.
3. She is more unhappy _____.
4. Smiling _____, she rushed to embrace them.
5. I am unable to join you _____.
6. Driving _____ is difficult.
7. _____, I will appear at the rally.
8. The meeting ended much sooner _____.
9. We decided to protest _____.
10. _____, we will try once again.

NAME _____ CLASS _____ DATE _____

3.3 | Clauses

Noun Clauses

A noun clause is a subordinate clause that acts as a noun.

USES OF NOUN CLAUSES	
Use	Example
Subject	*What his proposal will achieve* is anyone's guess.
Direct Object	I hope *that we will hear from you soon*.
Indirect Object	I told *whoever phoned* the news.
Object of a Preposition	Give them funds for *whatever they need*.
Predicate Nominative	A quick promotion is *what she expects*.
Appositive	Her plan, *that we improve the environment*, has much support.

EXERCISE A: Identifying Noun Clauses. Underline the noun clause in each sentence and tell how it is used.

EXAMPLE: Ted spoke about <u>what he likes</u>.   *object of a preposition*

1. We won't predict what the results will be. _____
2. How she appeared so suddenly is quite a mystery. _____
3. We gave whoever volunteered a list of instructions. _____
4. Grace's songs are about what she truly believes. _____
5. The company's goals are what we willll discuss now. _____
6. Whichever trip she chooses will be fine with us. _____
7. Bill's reply, that we remain firm, upset us all. _____
8. I will discuss the plan with whoever wishes to do so. _____
9. Her major problem is whether she can go at all. _____
10. I know how they will react to his allegation. _____

EXERCISE B: Writing Sentences with Noun Clauses. Add a noun clause to each sentence below.

EXAMPLE: He wondered   *what would happen next*   .

1. This rule, _____, cannot be enforced.
2. _____ is difficult to say at this time.
3. Of course, we hope _____.
4. His reason was _____.
5. The speaker told about _____.
6. We will bring _____ a sandwich and coffee.
7. I know _____
8. _____ is not easy to predict.
9. They were extremely proud of _____.
10. A trip to a warm climate is _____.

NAME _____ CLASS _____ DATE _____

3.4 Sentences Classified by Structure

The Four Structures of Sentences

English sentences may be classified by the number and kind of clauses they contain.

Kind of Sentence	Number and Kind of Clauses	Examples
Simple	One independent clause	Nicole's trip to Europe was delightful.
Compound	Two or more independent clauses (properly punctuated)	Brad explained his plans for the new park, and the residents reacted enthusiastically.
Complex	One independent clause and one or more subordinate clauses	Whenever I am in Boston, I like to visit Faneuil Hall.
Compound-Complex	Two or more independent clauses and one or more subordinate clauses	I write music as an avocation, and Ellen composes lyrics whenever she has the time.

EXERCISE A: Identifying the Structure of Sentences. Identify each sentence as (1) simple, (2) compound, (3) complex, or (4) compound-complex.

EXAMPLE: Her idea is both practical and original. __1__

1. Either Sally will speak, or we will send another representative. _____
2. At this time there are several desirable tours available. _____
3. When the warehouse exploded, everyone in the neighborhood was stunned. _____
4. The Battle of the Bulge was Hitler's last great offensive thrust in World War II. _____
5. Since the speaker had arrived, we began the opening ceremonies, but we were soon interrupted by a few late stragglers. _____
6. A four-color process is used in much printing; the four colors employed are blue, yellow, red, and black. _____
7. This is the actual room where Mozart wrote his music. _____
8. Granada in Spain is famous for its Muslim monuments. _____
9. Bradley will play for Portland if he receives a satisfactory contract. _____
10. We prepared the luncheon as soon as we arrived, and we finished none too soon. _____

EXERCISE B: Writing Different Types of Sentences. Follow the directions below.

1. Write a compound-complex sentence consisting of two independent clauses and one subordinate clause.

   _____

   _____

2. Write a compound sentence in which the second independent clause follows the word *or*.

   _____

3. Write a simple sentence beginning with the expletive *there*.

   _____

4. Write a complex sentence which contains an adjective clause.

   _____

5. Write a complex sentence which contains a noun clause.

   _____

3.5 Diagraming Phrases and Clauses

Prepositional Phrases

A prepositional phrase is diagramed directly beneath the word it modifies. The preposition goes on a slanted line and the object sits on a horizontal line. If a prepositional phrase modifies the object of a preposition in another phrase, it is diagramed directly under the object of the preposition of the first phrase.

ADJECTIVE PHRASES

A young couple *with children in tow* arrived late.

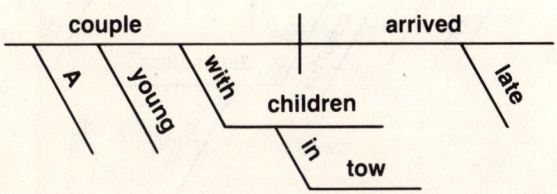

ADVERB PHRASES

A package came *for you* early *in the morning*.

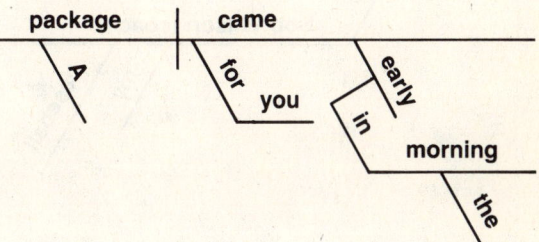

EXERCISE A: Diagraming Prepositional Phrases. Diagram the following sentences in the spaces below.

1. The singers from Italy and Germany were wonderful.
2. The car in the garage was damaged in the accident.

EXERCISE B: More Work with Diagrams. Correctly diagram each sentence.

1. These spices are bitter to the taste.
2. I will speak to the person in charge.

3.5 Diagraming Phrases and Clauses

Appositives and Appositive Phrases
Put an appositive in parentheses following the noun or pronoun it renames. Any modifiers go directly beneath it.

APPOSITIVE PHRASES

I spoke to Bob Wilson, *my baseball coach*.

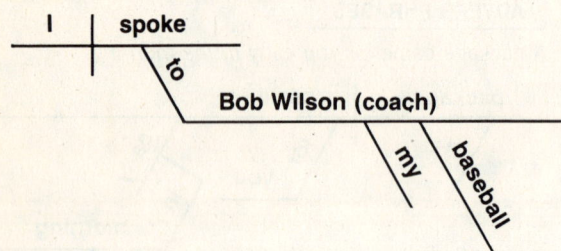

His poster, *a colorful drawing of modern Jerusalem*, is not accurate.

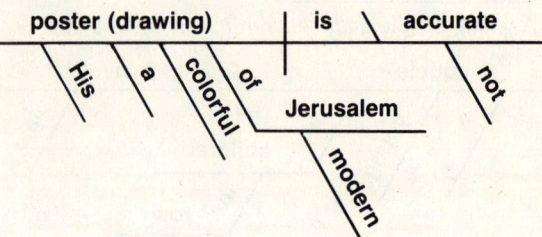

EXERCISE A: Diagraming Appositives and Appositive Phrases. Diagram the following sentences in the spaces below.

1. My new car, a sleek Mazda, is quite expensive.
2. I bought a warm shirt, a flannel with bright stripes.

EXERCISE B: More Work with Diagrams. Correctly diagram each sentence.

1. Harry Houdini, the famous magician, died in 1926.
2. The dancer was born in Hopkins, a city in Minnesota.

3.5 Diagraming Phrases and Clauses

Participles and Participial Phrases

A participle is placed directly beneath the noun or pronoun it modifies. Write it partly on a slanted line and partly on a horizontal line with any modifiers beneath it. A complement, such as a direct object, is placed on the horizontal line. A nominative absolute, formed from a noun and a participle, is positioned above the rest of the sentence as shown in the example on the right.

PARTICIPIAL PHRASE

The reporter, *telling a story to the police*, entered the building.

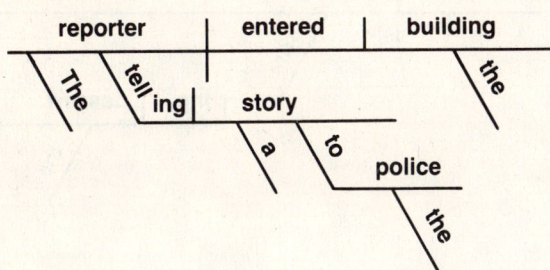

NOMINATIVE ABSOLUTE

Her mission finished, she returned to the city.

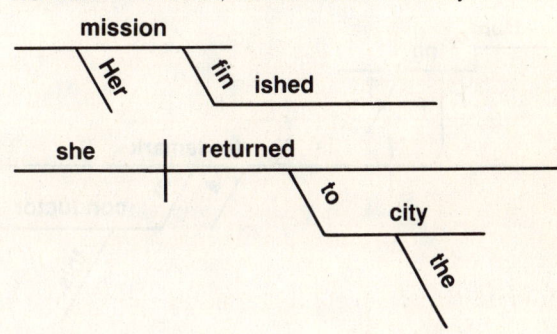

EXERCISE A: Diagraming Participles and Participial Phrases. Diagram the following sentences using the spaces provided.

1. Reaching the window, the woman called for help.

2. His car destroyed, Tom notified the police.

EXERCISE B: More Work with Diagrams. Correctly diagram each sentence.

1. The children, playing in the rain, ruined their shoes.

2. Frozen carefully, the turkey was ready for the oven.

3.5 Diagraming Phrases and Clauses

Gerunds and Gerund Phrases

Gerunds and gerund phrases used as subjects, direct objects, or predicate nominatives are placed on a stepped line atop a pedestal. Modifiers and complements are diagramed in the usual way. When a gerund or gerund phrase is used as an indirect object or object of a preposition, the stepped line extends from a slanted line.

GERUND PHRASES

Humming softly is a trademark of this conductor.

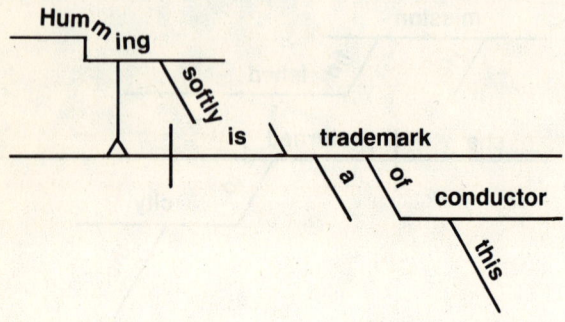

She was prevented from *eating the dessert*.

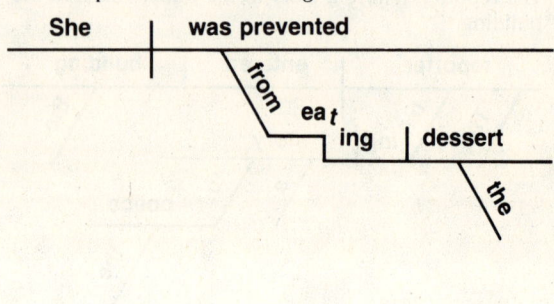

EXERCISE A: Diagraming Gerunds and Gerund Phrases. In the spaces provided below, diagram the following sentences.

1. Basking in the sun is her favorite activity.
2. I often remember waiting at his house.

EXERCISE B: More Work with Diagrams. Correctly diagram each sentence.

1. My uncle relaxes by painting landscapes.
2. His major responsibility is preparing a schedule of activities.

3.5 Diagraming Phrases and Clauses

Infinitives and Infinitive Phrases

Infinitives are diagramed in several different ways. An infinitive used as a noun is diagramed on a pedestal. When an infinitive acts as an adjective or adverb, its diagram is similar to that of a prepositional phrase. The subject of an infinitive is placed on a line to the left. An understood *to* is placed in parentheses.

INFINITIVE PHRASES

To listen to opera is her hobby.

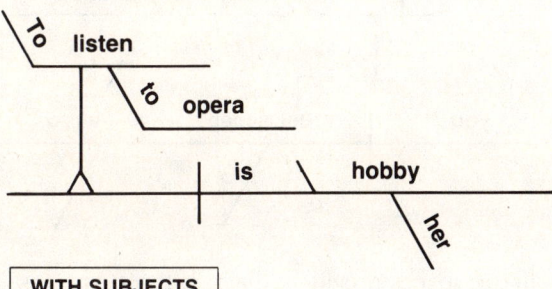

The best way *to reach the station* has been closed.

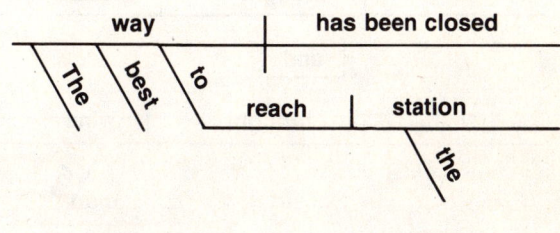

WITH SUBJECTS

Everyone expected *Chris to win the prize*.

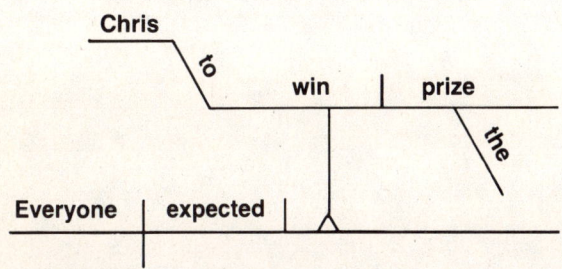

We saw *Bill open the present*.

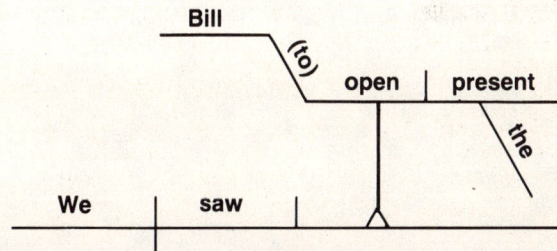

EXERCISE A: Diagraming Infinitives and Infinitive Phrases. Diagram the following sentences in the spaces provided.

1. We watched Terry swim the channel.
2. The reason to read newspapers is obvious.

EXERCISE B: More Work with Diagrams. Correctly diagram each sentence.

1. Jean's role is to monitor the performance.
2. To fly to Denver is the best way.

3.5 Diagraming Phrases and Clauses

Compound Sentences

Diagram each independent clause of a compound sentence as you would a separate sentence. Then join the verbs of the clauses with a dotted step line. On the step line, write either the coordinating conjunction or the semicolon that joins the two clauses.

COMPOUND SENTENCES

Phil brought the pizza, and Nell brought the wine.   I have no explanation; you must accept my word now.

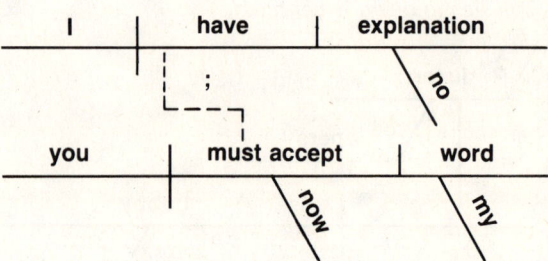

EXERCISE A: Diagraming Compound Sentences. In the spaces provided, diagram the sentences below.

1. The train arrived early, but we were waiting at the station.

2. I already know your answer; you will refuse my request.

EXERCISE B: More Work with Diagrams. Correctly diagram each sentence.

1. Most of London was destroyed in the war, but every important building has been restored.

2. She read the recipe carefully; then she assembled the ingredients.

3.5 Diagraming Phrases and Clauses

Complex Sentences

Both adjective and adverb clauses are diagramed on a line beneath the independent clause and connected to the independent clauses by a dotted line. With an adjective clause, the dotted line extends from the noun or pronoun the clause modifies to the relative pronoun or relative adverb in the clause. With an adverb clause, the dotted line extends from the word modified to the verb in the adverb clause. The subordinating conjunction is written along the dotted line.

ADJECTIVE CLAUSE

This is the clock *that you requested*.

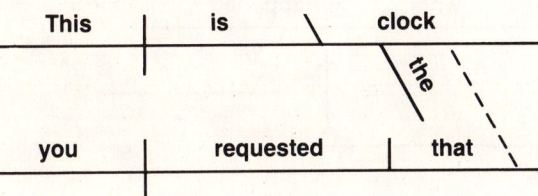

ADVERB CLAUSE

If you write to us, I will send you their address.

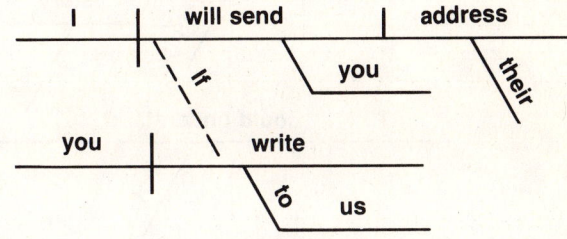

A noun clause is placed on a pedestal extending upward from the position it fills in the independent clause. If the introductory word has no function in the noun clause, it is written along the pedestal.

NOUN CLAUSES

I wonder *whether they are safe*.

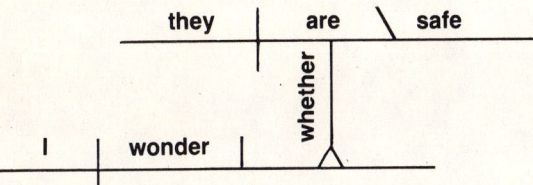

She writes best about *what she knows*.

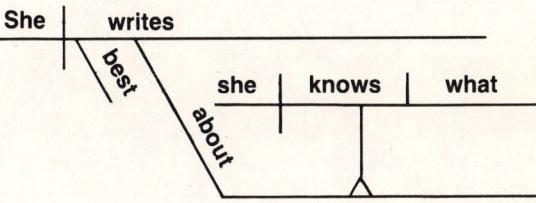

EXERCISE A: Diagraming Complex Sentences. Diagram the following sentences in the spaces provided.

1. I know what she means.

2. We arrived after the party began.

EXERCISE B: More Work with Diagrams. Correctly diagram each sentence.

1. The memo which he received explained the problem clearly.

2. Whichever hat she wants will be fine with us.

3.5 Diagraming Phrases and Clauses

Compound-Complex Sentences

To diagram a compound-complex sentence, begin by diagraming each of the independent clauses. Then diagram the subordinate clause(s).

COMPOUND-COMPLEX SENTENCE

I carefully listened to her story, but I could not understand what happened to her.

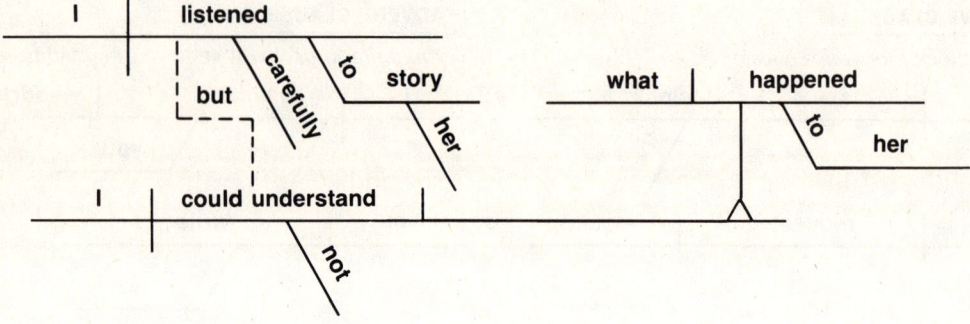

EXERCISE A: Diagraming Compound-Complex Sentences. Diagram the following sentences in the spaces provided.

1. Betty received the camera that she wanted, and she is eager to use it.

2. Since the plane was grounded, the passengers lost hope, and many left for home.

EXERCISE B: More Work with Diagrams. Correctly diagram each sentence.

1. I read the book which my teacher recommended, and I liked it very much.

2. The injured quarterback wanted to remain in the game, but he was forced to come out because the pain was unbearable.

NAME _____ CLASS _____ DATE _____

4.1 Fragments and Run-ons

Fragments

Do not capitalize and punctuate phrases, subordinate clauses, or words in a series as if they were complete sentences.

Fragments	Complete Sentences
At the approach of sunset.	We returned to shore *at the approach of sunset*.
Disturbed by the shouting.	Everyone was *disturbed by the shouting*.
A car, a bus, or a plane.	You have a choice of *a car, a bus, or a plane*.
When she spoke to us later.	*When she spoke to us later*, she changed her mind.
Which is in the next county.	Christy's, *which is in the next county*, is a fine restaurant.

EXERCISE A: Distinguishing Between Fragments and Complete Sentences. Write *F* if the group of words is a fragment and *S* if it is a complete sentence.

EXAMPLE: Waiting for hours at the bus terminal. *F*

1. The northern road from Barcelona. _____
2. Whether he intends to follow through on his threat. _____
3. The committee discussed a school anniversary celebration. _____
4. Within minutes of the appearance of the first flash. _____
5. A glass of orange juice, Belgian waffles, and coffee. _____
6. Frightened by an early morning phone call. _____
7. Unfortunately, the package was shipped to the wrong address. _____
8. She likes to read novels of espionage. _____
9. Which can be found in any reputable reference book. _____
10. Asked for and received a second opportunity. _____

EXERCISE B: Changing Fragments into Complete Sentences. Each group of words below is a fragment. Add whatever is necessary to make it into a complete sentence. Then draw a single line under the subject, and a double line under the verb.

EXAMPLE: Adjusting the turntable again.
 Adjusting the turntable again, I finally got it right.

1. Reaching the stop sign. _____
2. A chisel, a hammer, and headless nails. _____
3. If you phone her. _____
4. Between you and me. _____
5. Frozen together. _____
6. In the reference section of the school library. _____
7. Since she fell. _____
8. With rubber cement. _____
9. Which Mother wanted. _____
10. In the file cabinet. _____

NAME _____ CLASS _____ DATE _____

4.1 Fragments and Run-ons

Run-ons

A run-on sentence consists of two or more complete sentences that are not properly joined or separated. Use punctuation, conjunctions, or other means to separate the parts of a run-on sentence correctly.

Run-on Sentences	Properly Punctuated Sentences
Jason plays football, Jeff prefers soccer and track.	Jason plays football, and Jeff prefers soccer and track.
The first bus was an hour late the second was on time.	The first bus was an hour late; the second was on time.
Jo Ann never cared for city life, I just don't know why.	Jo Ann never cared for city life. I just don't know why.

EXERCISE A: Distinguishing Between Run-ons and Properly Punctuated Sentences. If the sentence is a run-on, write *RO;* if the sentence is correct, write *S*.

EXAMPLE: The road curved sharply, she swerved into a fence.   *RO*

1. Dave is a computer whiz, he is also a crackerjack programmer. _____
2. Brahms wrote four symphonies each one is superb. _____
3. From the oven came an aroma of chocolate and honey. _____
4. Mickey is an expert seamstress, she makes her own clothes. _____
5. Some companies manufacture special security envelopes. _____
6. Charles researched the topic, and later he wrote the brief. _____
7. There are three possibilities I don't like any of them. _____
8. Steve has grown massive, his doctor wants him to lose weight. _____
9. Zimbabwe used to be called Rhodesia, the old capital Salisbury is now called Harare. _____
10. Judy types daily she is trying to finish a research paper. _____

EXERCISE B: Changing Run-ons into Properly Punctuated Sentences. Rewrite each run-on so that it is correct.

EXAMPLE: I play second base, Bill is the shortstop.
         I play second base, and Bill is the shortstop.

1. There are two choices I will explain them both.
   _____

2. The new mall will contain sixty shops enclosed parking will be nearby.
   _____

3. Cabbage can be prepared in many ways, my favorite is stuffed cabbage.
   _____

4. Carl Sagan wrote *Cosmos* he also is the author of *Broca's Brain*.
   _____

5. Ice, of course, is dangerous, last winter Father slipped and fell.
   _____

4.2 Misplaced and Dangling Modifiers

Misplaced Modifiers

A misplaced modifier seems to modify the wrong word in a sentence. It should be placed as close as possible to the word it modifies.

MISPLACED MODIFIERS	
Misplaced	Improved
Gloria purchased a wristwatch in Chicago *with a leather band*.	In Chicago Gloria purchased a wristwatch *with a leather band*.
The map is in the hall closet *that you need*.	The map *that you need* is in the hall closet.

Dangling Modifiers

A dangling modifier seems to modify the wrong word or no word at all because the word it should modify has been omitted from the sentence.

DANGLING MODIFIERS	
Dangling	Improved
Reading the first paragraph, the book was too difficult.	*Reading the first paragraph*, I realized the book was too difficult.
While scoring the winning goal, his father's cheer could be heard clearly.	*While scoring the winning goal*, he heard his father's cheer clearly.

EXERCISE A: Recognizing Misplaced Modifiers. Underline each misplaced modifier.

EXAMPLE: The patrol car usually waits near the station <u>with the loud horn</u>.

1. The old woman bumped into the bench walking her dog.
2. Marie gave her TV to her younger sister with remote control.
3. The lithograph was a genuine Chagall that was stolen.
4. The girls fled from the dormitory noticeably upset.
5. Bill wants a hamburger and coffee cooked well done.
6. Apricots have a better flavor that come from California.
7. Father bought new glasses in the city with bifocals.
8. The oak tree was hit by lightning with a forked trunk.
9. Grandma called the police frightened by the strange noise.
10. The city has to be Boston with the large outdoor fruit and vegetable market.

EXERCISE B: Recognizing Dangling Modifiers. Underline each dangling modifier. If a sentence has no dangling modifier, leave it unmarked.

EXAMPLE: <u>Turning the corner</u>, a beautiful sunset could be seen.

1. Closing the car trunk, her keys had been misplaced.
2. Announcing the winners, Bob spoke in a hushed voice.
3. Reaching the intersection, an accident blocked the next street.
4. While opening the package, a mistake was inadvertently made.
5. Raising his baton, the conductor began the symphony.

NAME _____ CLASS _____ DATE _____

4.3 Faulty Parallelism

Recognizing the Correct Use of Parallelism

Parallelism is the placement of equal ideas in words, phrases, or clauses of similar types.

PARALLEL WORDS, PHRASES, AND CLAUSES
Words: This room seems *bright, spacious,* and *suitable.* *Phrases: Gathering the best spices* and *mixing them carefully* are important if you want this recipe to work. *Clauses:* I have no patience with *what you said* or with *what you did.*

Correcting Faulty Parallelism

Correct a sentence containing faulty parallelism by rewriting it so that each parallel idea is expressed in the same grammatical structure. Faulty parallelism can involve words, phrases, and clauses in a series as well as comparisons.

CORRECTING FAULTY PARALLELISM
Nonparallel: My sister likes *to jog, to swim,* and *dance.* *Parallel:* My sister likes *to jog, to swim,* and *to dance.* *Nonparallel:* He prefers a *sandwich* to *eating a full meal.* *Parallel:* He prefers a *sandwich* to a full *meal.*

EXERCISE A: Recognizing Parallel Structure. In each sentence below, underline the parallel structures.

EXAMPLE: I walk <u>to school</u> and then <u>to work</u>.

1. A person who gives charity and who helps others is rare indeed.
2. In his career he has been an accountant, an expediter, and a consultant.
3. Growing very slowly and then bursting into glorious color is a characteristic of that tropical plant.
4. I have had virtually no peace since my daughter left and since my oldest son returned.
5. After the accident, she sobbed, whimpered, and collapsed.
6. Maggie always sings in the shower, at the breakfast table, and at most other times.
7. We try to jog daily and to hike on weekends.
8. Her hobbies include refinishing furniture, repairing clocks, and constructing floral displays.
9. Ms. Ames, Mr. Paulson, and Dr. Phillip will all present seminars at the convention.
10. She was fascinated to learn that Joel writes sonnets and that I develop mobiles.

EXERCISE B: Recognizing Faulty Parallelism. Next to each sentence below write *FP* if there is faulty parallelism and *C* if the sentence is correct.

EXAMPLE: I enjoy reading magazines rather than to clean my room. ___FP___

1. Smoking, drinking, and to gamble should be avoided. _____
2. My mother would rather bake fresh bread than buying a packaged loaf. _____
3. I expect to drive to Providence, to see two friends, and to return this evening. _____
4. My teacher prefers a simple list of ideas to preparing a complicated Harvard outline. _____
5. She would rather return to our hotel than going to the stadium. _____

4.4 Faulty Coordination

Recognizing Faulty Coordination

Use *and* or other coordinating conjunctions only to connect related ideas of equal importance.

FAULTY COORDINATION
Leonard Warren was perhaps the greatest of all baritones, *and* he loved to play chess.
Wilson is our top computer analyst, *and* he lives not far from our main office.

Correcting Faulty Coordination

Revise sentences with faulty coordination by putting unrelated ideas into separate sentences or by putting a less important or subordinate idea into a subordinate clause or a phrase.

CORRECTING FAULTY COORDINATION
Faulty: Amelia Earhart won the love of many Americans through her courageous early flights, *and* she never returned from her last flight.
Better: Amelia Earhart won the love of many Americans through her courageous early flights. She never returned from her last flight.

EXERCISE A: Recognizing Faulty Coordination. For the five sentences below in which coordination is used correctly, write *C*. For the others, write *F* for faulty.

EXAMPLE: New housing is out of the reach of most young couples today, and my grandparents once owned a new home. *F*

1. Our first report was not complete, but the second is much better. _____
2. Charles Goodyear invented a vulcanization process for rubber, and I need a new pair of front tires. _____
3. The 14th Amendment to the Constitution was ratified in 1868, and we need a new constitution for our club. _____
4. My grandfather always enjoyed puttering around the house, and he now lives in Montana. _____
5. Nellie Tayloe Ross became the first woman governor of a state in 1925, and later she served as the first woman director of the United States Mint. _____

EXERCISE B: Correcting Faulty Coordination. Correct the faulty coordination in the sentences below.

EXAMPLE: It was obvious that the Johnsons needed more closet space, and they had six children.
It was obvious that the Johnsons needed more closet space. They had six children.

1. World War II brought out a high degree of patriotism, and the war lasted for half a decade.

2. I have read a number of mystery stories, and all of them have been popular for years.

3. Our principal has just instituted a new behavior code, and she is married and has two children.

4. Australia is located in the Southern Hemisphere, and most countries are located in the Northern Hemisphere.

5. I plan to study architecture in college, but I also have a nervous stomach.

5.1 The Varieties of English

Standard English

Standard English may be formal or informal. Formal English uses the traditional standards of correctness. It is characterized by elaborate sentence structures and an extensive vocabulary. Informal English is conversational in tone. It uses a smaller vocabulary than formal English and generally shorter sentences.

Formal English	Informal English
In spite of all his hard work, the gardener could not conquer the ever-encroaching weeds.	The gardener just couldn't keep up with the weeds.

Nonstandard English

Nonstandard English may be either slang or dialect. Slang is a nonstandard form of English that is generally colorful and expressive but short-lived. Dialect is a nonstandard form of English that makes use of words, pronunciations, and sentence structures not commonly found in standard English.

Slang	Dialect
Uncle Max has a real hang-up about crossing bridges.	I reckon the little fella's plum tuckered out.

EXERCISE A: Recognizing Varieties of Standard English. Label each item F (formal) or I (informal).

EXAMPLE: I was appalled by his ignorance. __F__

1. The judge instructed the jurors about the technicalities of the law. _____
2. They're the two best players on the team. _____
3. We gazed out at the dark, ominous clouds looming in the distance. _____
4. All the other guests at the party felt his pretentious attitude was quite distasteful. _____
5. Mary's trying really hard to get her paper done. _____

EXERCISE B: Recognizing Varieties of Nonstandard English. Label each item S (slang) or D (dialect).

EXAMPLE: Jack's real ticked off at his little brother. __S__

1. It ain't no cat can't get in no coop. _____
2. My English teacher is a real cool dude. _____
3. Granny Hawkins took and put the eggs in her poke. _____
4. I's gonna get me some fancy clothes and take me out on the town. _____
5. Mrs. Smith has really been getting on my case about being late to class. _____

NAME _____ CLASS _____ DATE _____

5.2 | The History of English

Three Periods of Language Growth

The development of the English Language is divided into Old English, Middle English, and Modern English.

WORDS OF OLD-ENGLISH ORIGIN		
folk	house	work
live	eat	meat

In the several hundred years since the first English colonists arrived in America, American English has become increasingly different from British English.

American Usage	British Usage
oatmeal	porridge
washcloth	face flannel
flashlight	torch

EXERCISE A: Discovering Periods of Origin. Using a dictionary that provides etymologies, identify whether each of the following words was introduced into the English language during the Old English, Middle English, or Modern English periods.

EXAMPLE: labor _Middle English_

1. knock _____
2. grammar _____
3. divine _____
4. skid _____
5. pouch _____
6. chief _____
7. needle _____
8. side _____
9. professor _____
10. product _____

EXERCISE B: Distinguishing Between British and American Usage. In each sentence below, underline the word or expression from British English. Write the American English replacement on the line at the right, using a dictionary if necessary.

EXAMPLE: Will you please post this letter for me? _mail_

1. The chips that came with my hamburger are cold. _____
2. Alison's perfect look was spoiled by the ladder in her stocking. _____
3. Tom wore a plaid waistcoat with his navy blue suit. _____
4. You will have to queue up with the others to get a ticket. _____
5. The applicant had seen the advert in the morning paper. _____

NAME _____ CLASS _____ DATE _____

6.1 Verb Tenses

The Six Verb Tenses

A tense is a form of a verb that shows the time of an action or state of being. There are six different tenses, each with a basic and a progressive form. The present and past tenses also have an emphatic form.

Tenses	Basic Forms	Progressive Forms	Emphatic Forms
Present	I see	I am seeing	I do see
Past	I saw	I was seeing	I did see
Future	I will see	I will be seeing	
Present Perfect	I have seen	I have been seeing	
Past Perfect	I had seen	I had been seeing	
Future Perfect	I will have seen	I will have been seeing	

The Four Principal Parts

A verb has four principal parts: the present, the present participle, the past, and the past participle.

THE FOUR PRINCIPAL PARTS			
Present	Present Participle	Past	Past Participle
propel	propelling	propelled	(have) propelled
take	taking	took	(have) taken

EXERCISE A: Recognizing Tenses and Forms of Verbs. Underline the verb or verb phrase in each sentence below. Then write the tense and form of the verb.

EXAMPLE: The Pandas <u>were winning</u> in the first quarter. ___past progressive___

1. often study in the library. _____
2. The governor will be speaking to the Chamber of Commerce today. _____
3. The train arrived an hour late. _____
4. A few of the members did support my proposal. _____
5. We had been planning a picnic. _____
6. Lenore has finished her term paper already. _____
7. By the end of the run, the play will have had 12,500 performances. _____
8. Most of my friends do take their schoolwork seriously. _____
9. Some candidates will promise anything at election time _____
10. I am having a hard time understanding Max's anger. _____

EXERCISE B: Recognizing Principal Parts. On the lines below, write the principal part used to form the verb in each sentence above. Then write the name of that principal part.

EXAMPLE: ___winning present participle___

1. _____   6. _____
2. _____   7. _____
3. _____   8. _____
4. _____   9. _____
5. _____   10. _____

6.1 Verb Tenses

Regular and Irregular Verbs

A regular verb is one whose past and past participle are formed by adding -ed or -d to the present form.

PRINCIPAL PARTS OF REGULAR VERBS			
Present	**Present Participle**	**Past**	**Past Participle**
invent	inventing	invented	(have) invented
allege	alleging	alleged	(have) alleged
frighten	frightening	frightened	(have) frightened

An irregular verb is one whose past and past participle are not formed by adding -ed or -d to the present form.

PRINCIPAL PARTS OF IRREGULAR VERBS			
Present	**Present Participle**	**Past**	**Past Participle**
cost	costing	cost	(have) cost
catch	catching	caught	(have) caught
leave	leaving	left	(have) left
become	becoming	became	(have) become
break	breaking	broke	(have) broken
swim	swimming	swam	(have) swum

EXERCISE A: Writing the Principal Parts of Irregular Verbs. Add the missing principal parts.

EXAMPLE: ring   _ringing_   _rang_   _(have) rung_

1. _____   drinking   _____   _____
2. grow   _____   _____   _____
3. bite   _____   _____   _____
4. _____   _____   flew   _____
5. _____   hurting   _____   _____
6. _____   _____   _____   (have) slain
7. _____   speaking   _____   _____
8. _____   _____   _____   (have) frozen
9. draw   _____   _____   _____
10. _____   _____   rode   _____

EXERCISE B: Choosing the Correct Form of Irregular Verbs. Fill in each blank with the correct verb form from those given in parentheses.

EXAMPLE: Tanya has not yet _chosen_ her courses for next year. (chose, chosen)

1. Seveal large branches have _____ across the driveway. (chose, chosen)
2. I'm not sure I _____ the car door. (shut, shutted, shutten)
3. I have _____ my applications to three colleges. (send, sended, sent)
4. The neighbors _____ a huge party last night. (gave, given)
5. In the course of the experiment, the test tube _____. (burst, busted)

Copyright © by Prentice-Hall, Inc.

51

NAME _____ CLASS _____ DATE _____

6.1 Verb Tenses

Verb Conjugation

A conjugation is a complete list of the singular and plural forms of a verb. A short conjugation lists just the forms that are used with a single pronoun. As you study the following short conjugations, note that the verbs used with *you* are also used with *we* and *they*. The verbs used with *she*, likewise, are also used with *he* and *it*.

SHORT CONJUGATIONS			
Basic, Progressive, and Emphatic Forms	run (with *I*)	run (with *you*)	run (with *she*)
Present	I run	you run	she runs
Past	I ran	you ran	she ran
Future	I will run	you will run	she will run
Present Perfect	I have run	you have run	she has run
Past Perfect	I had run	you had run	she had run
Future Perfect	I will have run	you will have run	she will have run
Present Progressive	I am running	you are running	she is running
Past Progressive	I was running	you were running	she was running
Future Progressive	I will be running	you will be running	she will be running
Present Perfect Progressive	I have been running	you have been running	she has been running
Past Perfect Progressive	I had been running	you had been running	she had been running
Future Perfect Progressive	I will have been running	you will have been running	she will have been running
Present Emphatic	I do run	you do run	she does run
Past Emphatic	I did run	you did run	she did run

EXERCISE A: Conjugating Basic and Progressive Forms. Write a short conjugation for each item given below.

1. win (with *I*)   2. know (with *he*)   3. ride (with *we*)   4. love (with *they*)

_____   _____   _____   _____
_____   _____   _____   _____
_____   _____   _____   _____
_____   _____   _____   _____
_____   _____   _____   _____
_____   _____   _____   _____
_____   _____   _____   _____
_____   _____   _____   _____
_____   _____   _____   _____
_____   _____   _____   _____
_____   _____   _____   _____
_____   _____   _____   _____

EXERCISE B: Supplying the Correct Verb Form. Fill in each blank with the form of the verb given in parentheses.

EXAMPLE: We ___*were hoping*___ for your cooperation. (*hope*, past progressive)

1. Tony _____ a Giants' fan all his life. (*be*, present perfect)
2. We _____ New Mexico this summer. (*visit*, future progressive)
3. You _____ to help us. (*promise*, past emphatic)
4. Tomorrow we _____ here a month. (*live*, future perfect progressive)
5. We _____ soundly in spite of the noise. (*sleep*, past)

6.2 The Correct Use of Tenses

Present, Past, and Future Time

The three forms of the present tense show present actions or conditions as well as various continuous actions or conditions. The seven forms that express past time show actions or conditions beginning in the past. The four forms that express future time show future actions or conditions.

USES OF TENSE IN PRESENT TIME		
Verb Forms	**Use**	**Examples**
Present	present event	I *have* a headache.
	recurring event	Lou often *misses* the bus.
	constant event	The sun *rises* in the east.
Pres. Progressive	continuing event	Pam *is putting* the baby to bed.
Pres. Emphatic	emphasized event	We *do need* milk.
USES OF TENSES IN PAST TIME		
Past	completed event	Everyone *was* hungry.
Present Perfect	complete (indef. time)	Ed *has finished* his homework.
	continuing to present	The owner *has offered* a reward.
Past Perfect	completed before another past event	The snow *had stopped* before we began our trip.
Past Progressive	continuing past event	The wind *was blowing* from the west.
Present Perfect Progressive	continuing to present	The police *have been investigating* for several months.
Past Perfect Progressive	continuous before another past event	Carol *had been studying* when the power went off.
Past Emphatic	emphasized event	I *did give* you the phone message.
USES OF TENSES IN FUTURE TIME		
Future	future event	Dinner *will be* ready in a few minutes.
Future Perfect	future event before another future event	The agent *will have mailed* your tickets before the end of the week.
Future Progressive	continuing future event	The show *will be playing* for another week.
Future Perfect Progressive	continuous before another future event	In January we *will have been living* in this house for seven years.

EXERCISE A: Identifying Tenses. Underline each verb that shows present time. Circle each verb that shows past time. Put parentheses around verbs that show future time.

EXAMPLE: The press is following the case very closely. _____

1. In her youth, the pianist had studied with a famous composer. _____
2. The committee will have made its decision by tomorrow. _____
3. We did try to reach you last weekend. _____
4. Ed has been studying harder this term. _____
5. Crustaceans have the ability to regenerate lost claws. _____
6. This time next week, we will be lying on the beach in Jamaica. _____
7. A heavy fog was rolling in. _____
8. The travel agent will make all the reservations. _____
9. The contestant had answered only one question by the end of the show. _____
10. The train will be leaving from Track 8. _____

EXERCISE B: Identifying Uses of Verbs. In the space to the right of each sentence in Exercise A, write the use of the verb, using the labels in the chart.

EXAMPLE: The press is following the case very closely. *continuing event*

6.2 The Correct Use of Tenses

Sequence of Tenses

When showing a sequence of events, do not shift tenses unnecessarily. The tense of a verb in a subordinate clause should follow logically from the tense of the main verb.

SEQUENCE OF TENSES		
Main Verb	**Subordinate Verb**	**Type of Events**
I *know*	that you *are going* to Boston.	Simultaneous events
I *know*	that you *will help*.	Sequential events
I *knew*	that I *was* not wrong.	Simultaneous events
I *knew*	that the phone *had rung*.	Sequential events
We *will see*	if he *knows* the answer.	Simultaneous events (present used as future)
You *will see*	that you *have chosen* well.	Sequential events

The form of a participle or infinitive should set up a logical time sequence in relation to the main verb.

SIMULTANEOUS EVENTS		
Present	*Hearing* a siren, we *pull* over.	I *want to pay* you a visit.
Past	*Hearing* a siren, we *pulled* over.	I *wanted to pay* you a visit.
Future	*Hearing* a siren, we *will pull* over.	I *will want to pay* you a visit.
SEQUENTIAL EVENTS		
Present	*Having eaten*, we *leave* the table.	We *are* glad *to have been asked*.
Past	*Having eaten*, we *left* the table.	We *were* glad *to have been asked*.
Future	*Having eaten*, we *will leave* the table.	We *will be* glad *to have been asked*.

Modifiers That Help Clarify Tense

Use modifiers that indicate time to help clarify tense.

EXERCISE A: Using the Correct Tense. Begin or complete each of the following sentences with words of your own choice. Make sure that the verb you use works well with the other verb.

EXAMPLE: We will go to school after ___*we have eaten breakfast.*___

1. John feels that _____.
2. _____ that we had more time to complete this project.
3. I wrote to Steven while _____.
4. Tina sat at her desk and _____.
5. It has been several years since _____.

EXERCISE B: Adding Modifiers to Help Clarify Tense. Complete each of the sentences below by writing a modifier that clarifies time.

EXAMPLE: My parents are going to Europe ___*next month*___.

1. Phyllis has asked me to help her with her math homework _____.
2. The Tigers won the World Series _____.
3. My English class is _____ very interesting.
4. The _____ winters have been very long and cold.
5. _____, my father wakes up at 6:00.

6.3 The Subjunctive Mood

The Correct Use of the Subjunctive Mood

Use the subjunctive mood (1) in clauses beginning with *if* or *that* to express an idea contrary to fact or (2) in clauses beginning with *that* to express a request, a demand, or a proposal.

USES OF THE SUBJUNCTIVE	
Ideas Contrary to Fact	**Requests, Demands, Proposals**
I wish that today *were* Friday. If I *were* rich, I would buy a yacht.	They requested that he *leave*. I demand that the package *be* ready.

Auxiliary Verbs That Help Express the Subjunctive Mood

Could, would, or *should* can be used to help a verb express the subjunctive mood. In the following chart, the sentences on the left contain the past subjunctive form of the verb *be: were*. The sentences on the right have been reworded with *could* and *would*.

THE SUBJUNCTIVE MOOD EXPRESSED THROUGH AUXILIARY VERBS	
If you *were* to help me, I would finish by noon. If you *were* more careful, the paint would not have spilled.	If you *could* help me, I would finish by noon. If you *would* be more careful, the paint would not have spilled.

EXERCISE A: Using the Subjunctive Mood. Rewrite each sentence, changing the verb that should be in the subjunctive mood to its correct form.

EXAMPLE: If I was in your place, I would be nervous.
 If I were in your place, I would be nervous.

1. It is essential that the committee keeps its findings secret.

2. The law requires that you are eighteen in order to vote.

3. The librarian asks that all books are back before vacation.

4. I wish that I was going along.

EXERCISE B: Using Auxiliary Verbs to Express the Subjunctive Mood. Each of the following sentences contains a subjunctive verb used correctly. Rewrite each sentence, using an auxiliary verb to help express the subjunctive mood.

EXAMPLE: If you were to leave, I would be unhappy.
 If you should leave, I would be unhappy.

1. If I were neater, I would not have to rewrite this paper.

2. The kitchen would be cooler if you were to turn off the oven.

3. If you were to go to New York City, what would you want to see?

4. I would make a roast if you were to stay for dinner.

6.4 Voice

Active and Passive Voice

Voice is a form of a verb that shows whether the subject is performing the action. A verb is active if its subject performs the action. A verb is passive if its action is performed upon the subject. A passive verb is made from a form of *be* plus the past participle of a transitive verb.

Active Voice	Passive Voice
The early frost *damaged* the crops.	The crops *were damaged* by early frost.

Using Active and Passive Voice

Use the active voice whenever possible. Use the passive voice to emphasize the receiver of an action rather than the performer of an action. Also use the passive to point out the receiver of an action whenever the performer is not important or not easily identified.

Emphasizing the Receiver	Performer Unknown or Unimportant
Only Reggie *was amazed* by her actions after class.	This cheese *was imported* from Denmark. One name *was omitted* from the list.

EXERCISE A: Distinguishing Between Active and Passive Voice. After each sentence, write *active* or *passive* to describe the verb.

EXAMPLE: The ingredients should be blended slowly. ___passive___

1. Four large pizzas were delivered to us by mistake. _____
2. The new law protects consumers from unscrupulous dealers. _____
3. After some argument, Shandy agreed to rewrite the last act. _____
4. The nominee was elected by a voice vote. _____
5. The wind blew down several trees in the neighborhood. _____

EXERCISE B: Using the Active and Passive Voice. Write *weak* after each of the passive sentences below that would be more forceful in the active voice. Write *acceptable* after each sentence that makes good use of the passive voice.

EXAMPLE: Flight 21 has been delayed because of bad weather. ___acceptable___
The party was enjoyed by everyone. ___weak___

1. Browning's first book of poems was published anonymously. _____
2. My composition was given a C by Mrs. Morrison. _____
3. Tryouts will be held on Friday at 4 P.M. _____
4. The performance will be repeated tomorrow night. _____
5. The shoreline was battered by Hurricane Ida. _____

NAME _____ CLASS _____ DATE _____

7.1 Case

The Three Cases

Case is the form of a noun or pronoun that indicates its use in a sentence. The three cases are the nominative, the objective, and the possessive. Pronouns have different forms for all three cases. Nouns change form only in the possessive case.

Case	Use in Sentence	Forms
Nominative	subject, predicate nominative	I; you; he, she, it; we; they; player, players
Objective	direct object, indirect object, object of a preposition	me; you; him, her, it; us; them; player, players
Possessive	to show ownership	my, mine; your, yours; his; her, hers; its; our, ours; their, theirs; player's, players'

EXERCISE A: Identifying Case. Write the case of each underlined noun or pronoun in the following sentences.

EXAMPLE: The sandwich with a toothpick in it is <u>yours</u>. ____*possessive*____

1. Kevin borrowed some money from Jake and <u>me</u>. _____
2. <u>We</u> promised to visit again soon. _____
3. The first person we asked was <u>she</u>. _____
4. The <u>producers'</u> investment earned them a handsome profit. _____
5. Alice maintains that the idea was <u>hers</u> alone. _____
6. <u>Their</u> right to the property is incontestable. _____
7. The hot-air balloon lifted <u>its</u> cargo high above the spectators. _____
8. Did you follow <u>Aunt Vera's</u> recipe exactly? _____
9. Did you buy these pies or make <u>them</u> yourself? _____
10. The house with the flagpole in front is <u>ours</u>. _____

EXERCISE B: Recognizing the Use of Nouns and Pronouns. After each number, write the use of each underlined noun or pronoun in Exercise A: *subject, predicate nominative, direct object, indirect object, object of a preposition,* or *to show ownership*.

EXAMPLE: ____*to show ownership*____

1. _____ 6. _____
2. _____ 7. _____
3. _____ 8. _____
4. _____ 9. _____
5. _____ 10. _____

7.1 Case

The Nominative Case

Use the nominative case for the subject of a verb, for a predicate nominative, and for the pronoun at the beginning of a nominative absolute.

USES OF NOMINATIVE PRONOUNS	
Subject	*She* ordered a pizza with anchovies.
Predicate Nominative	The man to the right of the microphone is *he*.
Nominative Absolute	*We* knowing the answer, Donna looked to us for help.

The Objective Case

Use the objective case for the object of any verb, preposition, or verbal or for the subject of an infinitive.

USES OF OBJECTIVE PRONOUNS	
Direct Object	Lou told Ann and *me* about the party.
	Finding *us* at home, the Holts stayed for a visit.
Indirect Object	Pam found Mom and *me* a place to stay.
Object of a Preposition	The house seems empty without *them*.
Subject of an Infinitive	Did you ask *her* to make a centerpiece?

EXERCISE A: Identifying Pronouns in the Nominative Case. Circle the pronoun in the nominative case to complete each sentence. Then indicate the use of the pronoun by writing *S* (subject), *PN* (predicate nominative), or *NA* (pronoun in nominative absolute).

EXAMPLE: The woman carrying the basket of flowers is ((she), her) ___PN___

1. It was (she, her) whom the boss promoted. _____
2. Is the town's oldest couple (they, them) or the Halberts? _____
3. My father and (he, him) have been friends since high school. _____
4. (He, Him) being short of funds, Lenny was eager for any job at all. _____
5. Both her sister and (she, her) have often sat for the Newtons. _____

EXERCISE B: Identifying Pronouns in the Objective Case. Circle the pronoun in the objective case to complete each sentence. Then indicate the pronoun's use as *DO* (direct object), *IO* (indirect object), *OP* (object of a preposition, or *SI* (subject of an infinitive).

EXAMPLE: Grandma asked (I, (me)) to set the table. ___SI___

1. We appreciated your taking (we, us) to the game. _____
2. My friends left for the game without (I, me). _____
3. Pa ordered (he, him) to feed the horses. _____
4. The committee asked Tom and (she, her) to give their reports. _____
5. We brought Grandpa and (she, her) a gift from our trip. _____
6. Looking at all the pies, I had trouble choosing among (they, them). _____
7. Their parents did everything to encourage Anna and (she, her). _____
8. Will their parents allow (they, them) to come with us? _____
9. Please ask (she, her) to join us for dinner. _____
10. The coach gave (I, me) another chance to try out. _____

NAME _____ CLASS _____ DATE _____

7.1 Case

Errors to Avoid with Possessive Pronouns

Use a possessive pronoun before a gerund.

POSSESSIVE PRONOUNS
The committee authorized *her* buying the equipment.
She appreciated *their* responding so quickly.

Do not use an apostrophe with any possessive pronoun since they already indicate ownership. Do not confuse a possessive pronoun with a contraction.

Possessive Pronoun	Contraction
The dog was pacing up and down in front of *its* dog house.	I wonder when *it's* going to stop raining.

EXERCISE A: Using Pronouns in the Possessive Case. Write the correct word from the parentheses to complete each sentence.

EXAMPLE: Dad complains about ___my___ playing the stereo so loud. (me, my)

1. The coach encouraged _____ entering the competition. (him, his)
2. The best proposal of all was _____. (theirs, their's)
3. The cause of _____ feeling so awful was simply motion sickness. (him, his)
4. Each of the tables has _____ own centerpiece. (its, it's)
5. My brother was nervous about _____ teaching him to drive. (me, my)
6. The first house on the left is _____. (hers, her's)
7. Surely the hostess appreciated _____ bringing the dessert. (you, your)
8. Dad agreed to _____ painting the house. (them, their)
9. No one objected to _____ inviting a friend along. (us, our)
10. Please take the rolls out of the oven when _____ done. (their, they're)

EXERCISE B: Using All Three Cases of Pronouns. Write the correct pronoun from the parentheses to complete each sentence.

EXAMPLE: My family approves of ___my___ going away to school. (me, my)

1. My brother and _____ have shared a room for years. (I, me)
2. _____ teaching Andy how to play baseball pleased us. (Him, His)
3. Dad wanted Heather and _____ to wait for the delivery. (she, her)
4. A barred owl can hunt in total darkness using only _____ hearing. (it's, its)
5. Jack never would have finished without help from Ann and _____. (I, me)
6. Which of the collages is _____? (your's, yours)
7. If anyone deserves to win, it is _____. (she, her)
8. It was _____ speaking to the reporter that angered the officer. (him, his)
9. _____ deciding to move came as a surprise to us. (They're, Their)
10. Neither Janice nor _____ heard anything unusual. (she, her)

NAME _____ CLASS _____ DATE _____

7.2 Special Problems with Pronouns

Using *Who* and *Whom* Correctly

Learn to recognize the various cases of *who* and *whom* and to use them correctly in sentences. *Who* and *whoever* are in the nominative case and are used as subjects and predicate nominatives. *Whom* and *whomever* are in the objective case and are used as direct objects and objects of prepositions. For the possessive case, use *whose*, not *who's*.

THE CASES OF *WHO* AND *WHOM*	
Nominative	*Who* gave you that information? Leave the package with *whoever* is at home. Everyone wondered *who* the winner would be.
Objective	*Whom* will you ask? Have you apologized to *whomever* you offended? *Whom* have you shown the pictures to?
Possessive	*Whose* house is big enough for the party?

Pronouns in Elliptical Clauses

In elliptical clauses beginning with *than* or *as*, use the form of the pronoun that you would use if the clause were fully stated.

Elliptical Clauses	Completed Clauses
Henry studied harder than ___?___. The game meant more to Sue than ___?___.	Henry studied harder than *I* [did]. The game meant more to Sue than [it meant to] *me*.

EXERCISE A: Using *Who* and *Whom* Correctly. Complete each sentence by writing *who*, *whom*, *whoever*, or *whomever*.

EXAMPLE: ___Whoever___ is on duty will accept the delivery.

1. We will accept help from _____ offers it.
2. The student _____ you reported has been suspended.
3. From _____ did you get your information?
4. Phil is a player _____ always does his best.
5. _____ told you that story has the facts mixed up.
6. I wonder _____ the mayor will support.
7. Did Jack say _____ was having the party?
8. _____ will the board nominate as treasurer?
9. Everyone _____ met Angela admired her.
10. Are there any applicants _____ we haven't seen yet?

EXERCISE B: Using Pronouns in Elliptical Clauses. Complete each sentence with an appropriate pronoun from the parentheses.

EXAMPLE: My sister is a better musician than ___I___. (I, me)

1. The test was harder for Carol than _____. (I, me)
2. Can you make better brownies than _____? (she, her)
3. Success means more to some people than _____. (she, her)
4. Jenny worked as hard as _____. (they, them)
5. Lou has a newer bike than _____. (he, him)

Copyright © by Prentice-Hall, Inc.

NAME _____ CLASS _____ DATE _____

8.1 | Subject and Verb Agreement

The Number of Nouns, Pronouns, and Verbs

Number refers to the two forms of a word: singular and plural. Singular words indicate one; plural words indicate more than one.

NUMBER OF WORDS			
Part of Speech	Singular	Plural	Singular or Plural
Nouns	analogy mouse	analogies mice	trout, reindeer, sheep
Pronouns	I, he, she, it	we, they	you
Verbs	am, is, was has, does, eats		(you, we, they) are, were (I, you, we, they) have, do, eat

Singular and Plural Subjects

A singular subject must have a singular verb. A plural subject must have a plural verb. A phrase or clause that interrupts a subject and its verb does not affect its subject-verb agreement.

SUBJECT-VERB AGREEMENT	
Singular	Plural
He plays basketball. The girl setting up the chairs is Ann.	We play touch football. The people helping her are ushers.

The antecedent of a relative pronoun determines its agreement with a verb.

Plural Antecedent	Singular Antecedent
He is one of those *people* who never rest.	He is the only *one* of those people who never rests.

EXERCISE A: Determining the Number of Words. Write *S* (singular), *P* (plural), or *both*.

EXAMPLE: you __both__

1. she _____
2. deer _____
3. has found _____
4. island _____
5. geese _____
6. open _____
7. moose _____
8. departs _____
9. learn _____
10. became _____

EXERCISE B: Making Subjects and Verbs Agree. Complete each sentence by writing the verb form from parentheses that agrees with the subject.

EXAMPLE: The message from Grandma and Grandpa __is__ on the desk. (is, are)

1. Recent heavy frosts _____ ruined the citrus crops. (has, have)
2. Mary is the only one of the swimmers who _____ a chance to make the all-state team. (has, have)
3. Our teacher, along with several others, _____ judging the essays. (is, are)
4. Which of the scouts is the one who _____ the map? (has, have)
5. The windows on the north side _____ thermal glass. (has, have)

Copyright © by Prentice-Hall, Inc.

8.1 Subject and Verb Agreement

Compound Subjects

Two or more singular subjects joined by *or* or *nor* must have a singular verb. Two or more plural subjects joined by *or* or *nor* must have a plural verb. If one or more singular subjects are joined to one or more plural subjects by *or* or *nor,* the subject closest to the verb determines agreement. A compound subject joined by *and* is generally plural.

AGREEMENT WITH COMPOUND SUBJECTS	
Joined by *or* or *nor*	The ambassador or another diplomat gladly *receives* visitors. Neither the President nor his staff members *are* attending. Neither cookies nor a candy bar *is* a healthful snack. Either fruit or vegetables *are* preferable.
Joined by *and*	Hemingway and Fitzgerald *were* friends in Paris. Chicken, meat, and fish *spoil* quickly if not refrigerated. Pancakes and sausage *is* the breakfast special. Each junior and senior *was* given a chance to try out.

EXERCISE A: Compound Subjects Joined by *Or* or *Nor*. Write the verb form from parentheses that agrees with the subject in each sentence.

EXAMPLE: A bed roll or a sleeping bag __is__ essential. (is, are)

1. Brioche or Beef Wellington _____ patience to make. (takes, take)
2. Neither they nor she _____ any intention of going. (has, have)
3. A plant or a flower arrangement _____ a touch of color. (adds, add)
4. Pasta, potato, or a salad _____ each entree. (accompanies, accompany)
5. Neither sheets nor a blanket _____ on the guest-room bed. (was, were)
6. Kevin, Tina, or Len _____ a copy of the article. (has, have)
7. Air conditioning or power steering _____ extra. (costs, cost)
8. Either custard or pudding _____ a nutritious dessert. (makes, make)
9. Neither Paula nor her children _____ to the neighbors. (speaks, speak)
10. Candles or a flashlight _____ with this job. (helps, help)

EXERCISE B: Compound Subjects Joined by *And*. Write the verb form from parentheses that agrees with the subject in each sentence.

EXAMPLE: Cream cheese and lox __is__ a popular deli item. (is, are)

1. Coral reefs and sudden squalls _____ serious hazards to small craft. (is, are)
2. Socks and sweaters _____ in that drawer. (goes, go)
3. Each boy and girl _____ given a favor to take home. (was, were)
4. Both Uncle Ben and Aunt Ella _____ on selling the house. (agrees, agree)
5. The hotel and some shops _____ at the end of the summer. (closes, close)
6. The park and the shopping mall _____ assets to the town. (is, are)
7. Fish and chips _____ a popular meal in British pubs. (is, are)
8. Scissors and paper _____ all that you need to make this. (is, are)
9. Every parent and child on the street _____ helped with the project. (has, have)
10. Both my sister and I _____ cooking. (enjoys, enjoy)

8.1 Subject and Verb Agreement

Confusing Subjects

Always check certain kinds of subjects carefully to make sure they agree with their verbs.

AGREEMENT WITH CONFUSING SUBJECTS	
Subject After Verb	There *is* only one direct *flight* daily. Beyond my personal objections *is* the *question* of the candidate's qualifications.
Subject Versus Predicate Nominative	My first *choice is* checkers. Tortilla *chips are* a good snack.
Collective Nouns	The *jury looks* sympathetic. The *jury have* rooms on the top floor of the hotel.
Plural Form with Singular Meaning	*Scabies is* caused by a mite. *Mathematics is* my favorite subject.
Amounts and Measurements	Three *days is* not enough time to finish our job. Eight *ounces equals* one cup.
Titles	*Green Eggs and Ham is* a popular children's book.
Indefinite Pronouns	*Either* of the houses *is* expensive. (always singular) *Many* in the group *were* disgruntled. (always plural) *Most* of the cheese *has* mold on it. *Most* of the apples *are* ripe now.

EXERCISE A: Deciding on the Number of Subjects. Assume that each item below is to be the subject of a sentence. Label each one *S* if it needs a singular verb or *P* if it needs a plural verb.

EXAMPLE: *Little Women* ___S___

1. Some of the cookies _____
2. Gymnastics _____
3. *Of Mice and Men* _____
4. Half of the crackers _____
5. Mumps _____
6. All of the money _____
7. *All the King's Men* _____
8. Physics _____
9. Neither of the speakers _____
10. Any of the fabric _____

EXERCISE B: Choosing Verbs to Agree with Difficult Subjects. Write the correct verb form from parentheses to complete each sentence.

EXAMPLE: There ___is___ no one home at the moment. (is, are)

1. The series of six lectures _____ next week. (begin, begins)
2. The panel _____ disagreeing on the rules. (is, are)
3. Among the old clothes _____ several usable sweaters. (is, are)
4. Three fourths of the records _____ scratched. (is, are)
5. The executive council _____ to make its decision tonight. (meets, meet)
6. All of the members of the family _____ present at the reunion. (was, were)
7. The least of the problems _____ where to have the party. (is, are)
8. Among the students, there _____ been little interest. (has, have)
9. *Romeo and Juliet* _____ a popular Shakespearean play. (remains, remain)
10. The orchestra _____ tuning their instruments. (is, are)

8.2 Pronoun and Antecedent Agreement

Agreement Between Personal Pronouns and Antecedents

A personal pronoun must agree with its antecedent in number, person, and gender. Use a singular personal pronoun with two or more singular antecedents joined by *or* or *nor*. Use a plural personal pronoun with two or more antecedents joined by *and*. Use a plural personal pronoun if any part of a compound antecedent joined by *or* or *nor* is plural. When dealing with pronoun-antecedent agreement, take care not to shift either person or gender. When gender is not specified, use the masculine or rewrite the sentence.

PRONOUN-ANTECEDENT AGREEMENT

Ben has misplaced *his* notecards.

This basketball has a leak in *it*.

Pam or Janice will have the party at *her* house.

The letter and the envelope have coffee stains on *them*.

Neither the guide nor the tourists could believe *their* eyes.

Every player must do *his* best.

All players must do *their* best.

EXERCISE A: Choosing Personal Pronouns to Agree with Antecedents. Assume that each item below is an antecedent for a personal pronoun. After each, write *his, her, its,* or *their* to show which pronoun you would use to refer to it.

EXAMPLE: My father or my uncle ___his___

1. most public speakers _____
2. the tape recorder _____
3. either Kevin or Marc _____
4. Grace, Maria, or Anna _____
5. only one waitress _____
6. Matthew or Carl _____
7. each boy in the club _____
8. both committees _____
9. the locker room _____
10. the famous soprano _____

EXERCISE B: Pronoun-Antecedent Agreement in Sentences. Write an appropriate personal pronoun to complete each sentence.

EXAMPLE: My brothers and I are planning a surprise for ___our___ parents.

1. Al is someone who uses _____ time wisely.
2. The food was so spicy that _____ burned my mouth.
3. Neither Sue nor Kathy had any trouble choosing _____ topic.
4. The doctor and her assistant have published _____ findings.
5. Harold hopes _____ application will get to the admissions office in time.
6. Ken is coaching _____ sister's softball team.
7. Several members are giving _____ time to work with senior citizens.
8. Mr. Simpson, _____ order is ready now.
9. Marcia has gotten a part-time job to help with _____ college expenses.
10. Either Hugh or Brian will volunteer _____ time for the food pick-up.

8.2 Pronoun and Antecedent Agreement

Agreement with Indefinite Pronouns

Use a singular personal personal pronoun when the antecedent is a singular indefinite pronoun. Use a plural personal pronoun when the antecedent is a plural indefinite pronoun. With an indefinite pronoun that can be either singular or plural, agreement depends on the antecedent of the indefinite pronoun.

AGREEMENT WITH INDEFINITE PRONOUNS
Each of the women brought *her* own specialty to the party.
Few of the neighbors have raked *their* leaves yet.
Some of the cupcakes have sprinkles on *them*. (*cupcakes* = plural antecedent)
Some of the lawn has dandelions in *it*. (*lawn* = singular antecedent)

Agreement with Reflexive Pronouns

A reflexive pronoun must agree with an antecedent that is clearly stated.

REFLEXIVE PRONOUN AGREEMENT	
Incorrect	**Correct**
Jason and *myself* enjoy the same kind of music.	Jason and *I* enjoy the same kind of music.

EXERCISE A: Making Personal Pronouns Agree with Indefinite Pronouns. Write an appropriate personal pronoun to complete each sentence.

EXAMPLE: Each of the Brownies has sold ___her___ quota of Girl Scout cookies.

1. Most of the fans brought blankets with _____.
2. Most of our furniture has scratches on _____.
3. Several of my classmates handed in _____ essays early.
4. No one on the girls' swim team wears _____ goggles in a meet.
5. Everyone in the Women's Club brings _____ own expertise to the project.
6. Few of the voters changed _____ minds after the debate.
7. Much of the glass has smudges on _____.
8. Has anyone in Dan's Cub Scout pack decided on _____ project yet?
9. All of the musicians are tuning _____ instruments.
10. I think some of the tourists brought cameras with _____.

EXERCISE B: Using Reflexive Pronouns Correctly. Underline the misused reflexive pronoun in each sentence. Write the correct pronoun on the line.

EXAMPLE: Please leave a message with Carlo or <u>himself</u>. ___him___

1. Gina or herself may be able to help you. _____
2. Don't forget to bring two sharpened pencils with yourself. _____
3. Kara and myself are on the decorations committee. _____
4. Pete will wear a jester's costume if ourselves can find one. _____
5. I loved the stories Grandma told yourself and me when we were little. _____

8.3 Special Problems with Pronoun Agreement

Vague Pronoun References

A pronoun requires an antecedent that is either clearly stated or clearly understood. The pronouns *which, this, that,* and *these* should not be used to refer to a vague or overly general idea. The personal pronouns *it, they,* and *you* should not be used with vague antecedents. Note that the use of *it* as a subject in such expressions as *It is raining* and *It is true* is acceptable and need not be avoided.

Vague Reference	Correct
Jake had good grades and was an outstanding athlete. He hoped *this* would help him get a scholarship.	Jake had good grades and was an outstanding athlete. He hoped *these factors* would help him get a scholarship.
In the paper, *it* says we had six inches of snow.	*The paper* reports that we had six inches of snow.
When visiting Paris, *you* can see the Eiffel Tower.	*Visitors to Paris* can see the Eiffel Tower.

EXERCISE A: Correcting Vague Pronoun References. Rewrite each sentence below to correct a vague reference involving *which, this, that,* or *these*.

EXAMPLE: We lost the game and it rained, which made us unhappy.
    We lost the game and it rained. Both events made us unhappy.

1. Jeff needs to improve his average and pass the final. This seems unlikely.

2. The boys promptly wrote thank-you notes, which shocked their mother.

3. Missy's boutique is the most successful shop in town. She deserves that.

4. Occasionally, we have a power failure or a bad storm. This frightens the children.

5. Many valuables were broken and some were lost, which makes me angry.

EXERCISE B: Solving More Problems with Pronoun References. Rewrite each sentence below that is faulty because of vague pronoun reference. If a sentence is correct as written, write *correct* in the space.

EXAMPLE: It was past midnight when the snow stopped.
    correct

1. At the annual picnic, they always feature barbecued chicken.

2. In that game, you can only reach "home" with an exact roll of the dice.

3. In Boston, they often drop their *r*'s.

4. It is just beginning to snow.

5. It suggests in the article that Perkins is guilty.

NAME _____ CLASS _____ DATE _____

8.3 Special Problems with Pronoun Agreement

Ambiguous Pronoun References

A personal pronoun should never refer to more than one antecedent. A personal pronoun should always be tied to a single, obvious antecedent.

Ambiguous Reference	Clear Reference
Angie told Faye that *she* had a flat tire.	Angie told Faye that *Faye* had a flat tire.

Do not repeat a personal pronoun if it can refer each time to a different antecedent.

Ambiguous Repetition	Correct
Phil told Jack that he would wait until after *his* football practice.	Phil told Jack that he would wait until after *Jack's* football practice.

Avoiding Distant Pronoun References

A personal pronoun should always be close enough to its antecedent to prevent confusion.

Distant Reference	Corrected
Teachers and counselors will be available in the senior lounge every Friday afternoon. All students are welcome to stop by. *They* will answer questions about schedules and curriculum.	Teachers and counselors will be available in the senior lounge every Friday afternoon. All students are welcome to stop by to ask questions about schedules and curriculum.

EXERCISE A: Recognizing Problems of Pronoun Reference. In the space at the right, write the antecedent of each underlined pronoun. If the pronoun has no single antecedent to which it clearly refers, write *FR* (for faulty reference) in the space.

EXAMPLE: Bill and Gary shared <u>his</u> lunch. ____FR____

1. After Nancy had spoken to Laura, <u>she</u> felt much calmer. _____
2. Mr. Pardi asked Tom to repeat the experiment <u>he</u> had just completed. _____
3. The still life was a masterpiece. The wine seemed to sparkle in the goblet, and the fruit looked real enough to eat. <u>It</u> made me gasp. _____
4. The approaches to the bridge were clogged, as <u>they</u> often were at rush hour. _____
5. The coach told Hankins that he would not renew <u>his</u> contract. _____

EXERCISE B: Correcting Problems of Pronoun Reference: Rewrite two of the items you marked *FR* in Exercise A, correcting the faulty reference.

EXAMPLE: *Bill and Gary shared Gary's lunch.*

1. _____
2. _____

9.1 Degrees of Comparison

Recognizing Degrees of Comparison

Most adjectives and adverbs have three different forms to show degrees of comparison.

DEGREES OF COMPARISON			
	Positive	**Comparative**	**Superlative**
Adjectives	ugly beautiful bad	uglier more beautiful worse	ugliest most beautiful worst
Adverbs	fast slowly badly	faster more slowly worse	fastest most slowly worst

Regular Forms

Use -er or *more* to form the comparative degree and -est or *most* to form the superlative degree of most one- and two-syllable modifiers. Use *more* and *most* to form the comparative and superlative degrees of all modifiers with three or more syllables.

REGULAR FORMS OF COMPARISON			
One- and two-syllable modifiers	sad happy tranquil	sadder happier more tranquil	saddest happiest most tranquil
Three or more syllables	sorrowful carefully	more sorrowful more carefully	most sorrowful most carefully

EXERCISE A: Recognizing Degrees of Comparison. Identify the degree of comparison of the underlined word in each sentence by writing *pos.* (positive), *comp.* (comparative), or *sup.* (superlative).

EXAMPLE: They have been waiting <u>longer</u> than we have.   *comp.*

1. The room will look <u>brighter</u> with a fresh coat of paint. _____
2. We congratulated the <u>proud</u> parents. _____
3. That was the <u>heaviest</u> rainfall on record. _____
4. Gretchen was voted <u>most likely</u> to succeed. _____
5. If I had been <u>more careful</u>, I wouldn't have made that mistake. _____
6. Casa Iguana serves the <u>spiciest</u> food in town. _____
7. The burglar moved <u>stealthily</u> along the balcony. _____
8. Surely the koala bear is one of the <u>laziest</u> animals. _____
9. An ice pack may make you feel <u>more comfortable</u>. _____
10. The stubborn child shook his head <u>vigorously</u>. _____

EXERCISE B: Comparing Adjectives and Adverbs. Write the missing forms of each modifier.

EXAMPLE: broad   *broader*   *broadest*

1. clever _____ _____
2. _____ _____ softest
3. _____ more unusual _____
4. friendly _____ _____
5. awkwardly _____ _____

9.1 Degrees of Comparison

Irregular Forms

The irregular comparative and superlative forms of certain adjectives and adverbs must be memorized.

IRREGULAR MODIFIERS		
Positive	**Comparative**	**Superlative**
bad	worse	worst
badly	worse	worst
far (distance)	farther	farthest
far (extent)	further	furthest
good	better	best
ill	worse	worst
late	later	last *or* latest
little (amount)	less	least
many	more	most
much	more	most
well	better	best

EXERCISE A: Forming Irregular Comparative and Superlative Degrees. Write the appropriate form of the modifier in parentheses to complete each sentence.

EXAMPLE: The hikers felt ___better___ after a short rest period. (good)

1. Students seldom do their _____ on tests when they are overtired. (well)
2. Max swam out _____ than he should have. (far)
3. That plant looks even _____ today than it did yesterday. (bad)
4. Of all the tourist attractions, we were _____ interested in seeing the White House. (little)
5. Her gown was in the _____ style. (late)
6. Only the second paragraph needs to be developed _____. (far)
7. Everyone agreed about who was the _____ player on the football team. (good)
8. People often feel even _____ on the second day of a cold than on the first. (ill)
9. Beginning musicians never play very well, but beginning violinists often play _____ of all. (badly)
10. We should have ordered _____ sandwiches for the party. (many)

EXERCISE B: Using Adjectives and Adverbs to Make Comparisons. Use each modifier in a sentence of your own to show a clear comparison. Use three comparative forms and two superlatives.

EXAMPLE: (much) ___This project is going to be more work than I thought.___

1. (bad) _____
2. (badly) _____
3. (good) _____
4. (many) _____
5. (well) _____

NAME _____ CLASS _____ DATE _____

9.2 Clear Comparisons

Using Comparative and Superlative Degrees

Use the comparative degree to compare two persons, places, or things. Use the superlative degree to compare three or more persons, places, or things.

Comparative (comparing two)	Superlative (comparing three or more)
Jerry studies *harder* than his brother.	Jerry studies *hardest* of the four children in the family.
The child moved *closer* to the horse.	That was the *closest* he had ever been to a large animal.

EXERCISE A: Using the Comparative and Superlative Degrees Correctly. Underline the correct form in each sentence.

EXAMPLE: If we had played (<u>more</u>, most) aggressively, we might have won.

1. Of all these movies, I have the (less, least) interest in seeing this one.
2. That watch is the (older, oldest) piece of jewelry in the collection.
3. Al should have proofread his essay (more, most) thoroughly.
4. Be sure to store the chicken in the (colder, coldest) part of the freezer.
5. The researchers will have to examine the specimen (more, most) closely.
6. That is the (more, most) delicate piece of needlework I have ever seen.
7. A speech for that audience should have a (more, most) formal tone.
8. Latin IV has the (fewer, fewest) students of any course.
9. The cheetah is the (faster, fastest) animal in the world.
10. This is the area of town I am (more, most) familiar with.

EXERCISE B: Recognizing Inappropriate Comparisons. In the sentences below, underline any problems that exist in comparisons. On the line below, rewrite each sentence correctly. If a sentence contains no errors, write *correct* on the line.

EXAMPLE: This is the <u>lovelier</u> party I have ever been to.
        This is the loveliest party I have ever been to.

1. Ben is happiest on his boat than on ours or the Petermans'.
   _____

2. Miguel seems to be the brightest of the twins.
   _____

3. The Jacobsons are the friendlier people on this block.
   _____

4. This is the lengthiest novel I have ever read.
   _____

5. I would be happier if you had chosen a safest route.
   _____

9.2 Clear Comparisons

Logical Comparisons

Make sure that your sentences compare only items of a similar kind.

Unbalanced Comparisons	Correct
Andre's car is newer than his mother.	Andre's car is newer than his mother's.
The damage from yesterday's rainstorm is greater than last month.	The damage from yesterday's rainstorm is greater than that from last month's.

When comparing one of a group with the rest of the group, make sure that your sentence contains the word *other* or the word *else*.

Illogical Comparisons	Correct
My grandmother is older than anyone in the family.	My grandmother is older than anyone else in the family.
Vincent's typing skills are greater than any student's in his class.	Vincent's typing skills are greater than any other student's in his class.

EXERCISE A: Making Balanced Comparisons. Rewrite each sentence, correcting the comparison.

EXAMPLE: Sue's dress is prettier than Jane.
Sue's dress is prettier than Jane's.

1. Your bonsai plant looks better than my mother.

2. Ted's bowl of spaghetti was bigger than his father.

3. The directions for putting together this model are more complicated than that model.

4. Frank's math test scores are higher than Judy.

5. Lenore's dress was less expensive than Janet.

EXERCISE B: Using *Other* and *Else* in Comparisons. Rewrite each sentence, correcting the comparison.

EXAMPLE: Mr. McMurty lived longer than anyone in his family.
Mr. McMurty lived longer than anyone else in his family.

1. Tom can throw farther than anyone on his team.

2. Brenda's report was more interesting than anyone's.

3. The boy who sits next to me speaks Spanish more fluently than anyone.

4. The flowers in this yard are prettier than any flowers on this street.

5. The Giants are better than any football team.

9.2 Clear Comparisons

Absolute Modifiers

Avoid using absolute modifiers illogically in comparisons.

Illogical	Correct
My glass is *fuller* than yours.	My glass is *more nearly full* than yours. My glass has *more in it* than yours.
I have never seen a *more spotless* house.	That is the only *spotless* house I have ever seen.

EXERCISE A: Correcting Illogical Comparisons. Rewrite each sentence, correcting any illogical comparisons.

EXAMPLE: Joan's opinions are the most opposite of mine.
Joan's opinions are the opposite of mine.

1. This model comes in a more infinite number of colors than that one.

2. Be sure the two posts are most perpendicular.

3. That snake has the most poisonous venom.

4. Mom should treat us more equally.

5. Try to make these two lines more parallel.

EXERCISE B: Writing Clear Comparisons. For each of the following items, write an effective comparison in one sentence.

EXAMPLE: Compare two of your favorite actresses.
Shirley MacLaine is a more dynamic actress than Debra Winger.

1. Compare two brands of cereal.

2. Compare the difference in weight between two of your friends.

3. Compare three of your favorite television programs.

4. Compare two animals found in a circus.

5. Compare what you had for dinner with what your friend had for dinner.

NAME _____ CLASS _____ DATE _____

10.1 Negative Sentences

Recognizing Double Negatives

Do not write sentences with double negatives.

CORRECTING DOUBLE NEGATIVES	
Double Negatives	**Corrections**
I *won't never* tell.	I *won't* ever tell.
	I will *never* tell.
Luis would*n't* let *no one* help him.	Luis would*n't* let anyone help him.
	Luis would let *no one* help him.
Michelle did*n't* know *nothing* about feeding chickens.	Michelle knew *nothing* about feeding chickens.
	Michelle did*n't* know anything about feeding chickens.

Forming Negative Sentences Correctly

Do not use two negative words in the same clause. Do not use *but* in its negative sense with another negative. Do not use *barely, hardly,* or *scarcely* with another negative word.

EXERCISE A: Recognizing Double Negatives. Label each sentence below as *DN* (containing a double negative) or *C* (correct).

EXAMPLE: Zach hadn't had no special training in scuba diving. ___DN___

1. Miss Conklin had not heard anything about a special program. _____
2. The guard hadn't seen nothing suspicious. _____
3. You can't find any better pet than a turtle. _____
4. The Number 4 bus no longer goes up Maple Avenue. _____
5. At first we couldn't see nothing in the darkness. _____
6. They don't have no more morning papers at the candy store. _____
7. The burglar didn't think of looking in the wastebasket. _____
8. The baby can't eat no more of those apples. _____
9. Neither of those boys has done anything wrong. _____
10. Ms. Martinez won't accept no late papers. _____

EXERCISE B: Correcting Double Negatives. Rewrite correctly five of the sentences you labeled *DN* in Exercise A.

EXAMPLE: *Zach hadn't had any special training in scuba diving.*

1. _____
2. _____
3. _____
4. _____
5. _____

NAME _____ CLASS _____ DATE _____

10.1 Negative Sentences

Understatement

Understatement can be achieved by using a negative word and a word with a negative prefix.

UNDERSTATEMENTS
The special investigator found that the mayor's conduct was *not improper*. Owen was *not unimpressed* with her command of Mongolian.

EXERCISE A: Using Understatement. Rewrite each sentence using understatement.

EXAMPLE: Dinner was expensive.   *Dinner was not inexpensive.*

1. The new crop of rookies was promising.

2. The climb is difficult, but possible.

3. The judge was sympathetic with the defendant's plight.

4. The extra cost of air conditioning is significant.

5. The reviews of the critics were enthusiastic.

EXERCISE B: Writing Negative Sentences. None of the following sentences contain negative words. Rewrite each sentence to express a negative idea.

EXAMPLE: Mr. Killerlane was pleased with my report.
Mr. Killerlane was displeased with my report.

1. It is easy for me to read the small print on the bottle.

2. Some of these pictures are mine.

3. Will was finished with his project.

4. Everybody came to the Miller's surprise party.

5. All the students bought the book.

NAME _____ CLASS _____ DATE _____

10.2 One Hundred Common Usage Problems

Solving Usage Problems

Study the items in the usage glossary in your textbook, paying particular attention to similar meanings and spellings, words that should never be used, pairs that are often misused, and problems with verb forms.

TYPES OF PROBLEMS		
Similar Spellings	beside, besides	all ready, already
Wrong Words	irregardless	nowheres
Misused Pairs	learn, teach	bring, take
Verb Forms	burst	have done

EXERCISE A: Avoiding Common Usage Problems. Underline the word(s) in parentheses that correctly complete each sentence.

EXAMPLE: Mr. Salvin (<u>burst</u>, busted) out laughing when he read my paper.

1. Who (beside, besides) you is planning to be absent?
2. The game was postponed (due to, because of) rain.
3. Boris's grandfather (learned, taught) him to play chess.
4. How is a dromedary different (from, than) a camel?
5. Chris was (eager, anxious) to begin working at her new job.
6. The rescue team was determined to go on (irregardless, regardless) of the risks.
7. Years of smoking will likely have a bad (affect, effect) on your lungs.
8. (Leave, Let) that poor cat alone!
9. Small animals (adapt, adopt) quickly to changes in their environment.
10. Buoyancy is an important (principal, principle) of physics.

EXERCISE B: Correcting Common Usage Problems. Underline the word or expression that creates a usage problem in each sentence below. Then correctly rewrite the sentence, using formal English.

EXAMPLE: The President <u>excepted</u> the challenge to debate.
   The President accepted the challenge to debate.

1. Nancy became real discouraged when the tenth publisher rejected her novel.

2. I done my homework already.

3. A slice of pizza is more healthy than a candy bar.

4. This here watch belonged to my great-grandfather.

5. The owner of this shop prides herself on her very unique selection of gifts.

11.1 Capitalization

Capitals for First Words

Use capital letters to begin words in each situation shown in the chart below.

Sentences	He is asleep.	Who called?
Interjection and Question Fragment	He took a terrible fall. Of course, I'll meet you.	Ghastly! But where?
Sentence in Quote	Didn't the sign say, "Trespassers will be prosecuted"?	
Sentence After Colon	The storm has halted traffic: Most roads are blocked.	
Lines of Most Poetry	Mary, Mary, quite contrary, How does your garden grow?	
Formal Resolutions	Resolved: That dues be increased by $1.00 per year.	
The Words *I* and *O*	Remember, O ye of little faith, I will return.	

Capitals for Proper Nouns

Capitalize each important word in all proper nouns, as shown below.

People/Animals: O.J. Simpson, Rover   *Place Names:* Oak Place, Eiffel Tower
Specific Events: the Iron Age, May Day   *Specific Groups:* Girl Scouts, Republicans
Religious Terms: Bible, Koran   *Awards:* Grammy, Golden Glove
Specific Craft: Model T. Concorde   *Brand Names:* Ford, Pepsi

Capitals for Proper Adjectives

Capitalize most proper adjectives.

Proper Adjectives with Capitals	Adjectives Without Capitals
Proper Nouns Used as Adjectives: French painter	*Common Terms:* french fries
Brand Names: Curad bandages	*Most Prefixes:* anti-American
Combinations: Anglo-Saxon poem	*Parts of Compounds:* German-made automobile

EXERCISE A: Using Capitals for First Words. Underline the word or words that should be capitalized in each of the following items.

EXAMPLE: <u>afterward</u> <u>i</u> remembered someone having said, "<u>watch</u> your step."

1. the first two lines of the poem are "tell me where is fancy bred, in the heart or in the head?"
2. we must find a way to help. but how?
3. what a silly thing that was to say! golly!
4. resolved: that students with straight *A*'s be exempt from taking mid-terms.
5. the driver exclaimed, "wow! that was a close call!"

EXERCISE B: Capitalizing Proper Nouns and Proper Adjectives. Underline each word or word part that should be capitalized in the sentences below.

EXAMPLE: the city of <u>montreal</u> has many <u>french</u>-speaking residents.

1. The halbert clinic accepts both blue cross and medicare patients.
2. The alhambra in granada is a famous example of moorish architecture.
3. Both the republican and the democratic candidates are hoping for a big win in new york.
4. This metroliner does not stop in metro park, new jersey.
5. Our neighbor, ellen blair, has just replaced her kodak with a polaroid.

11.1 Capitalization

Capitals for Titles
Capitalize titles of people and titles of works.

People	Works
Social: Lady Astor *Business:* Chairman Iacocca *Military:* General Westmoreland *Government:* Senator Watkins *Religious:* Archbishop Sheen *Compound:* Lieutenant Governor Hall *Abbreviations:* Mrs., Jr., Ph.D.	*Book:* All the King's Men *Periodical:* Reader's Digest *Poem:* "Birches" *Story:* "Shredni Vashtar" *Sculpture:* the Pietà *Composition:* The Seasons *Course:* Creative Writing II

Capitals in Letters
Capitalize the first word and all nouns in letter salutations and the first word in letter closings.

Salutations	Closings
My dear Friend, Dear Ambassador Parker:	With much love, Very truly yours,

EXERCISE A: Using Capitals in Titles. Underline the words that should be capitalized in each sentence.

EXAMPLE: Although it is somewhat dated, <u>*our hearts were young and gay*</u> still has its charm.

1. The young recruits dreaded sergeant Kerwin's temper.
2. The poem "the dry salvages" is the third of T. S. Eliot's *four quartets*.
3. The guest speaker will be senator Gerald Markham.
4. The course will be taught by Janet Saybrook, m.f.a.
5. I'm sure aunt Marnie would enjoy reading that book about general MacArthur.
6. Leonardo da Vinci painted both the *mona lisa* and *the last supper*.
7. On the feast of saint Francis, pastor Manners will bless the animals.
8. The publishers of *consumer reports* also publish *penny power* for young people.
9. One of the most popular songs from *annie* is "tomorrow."
10. Next semester, mr. Polari will teach poetry II.

EXERCISE B: Using Capitals for Salutations and Closings. Rewrite each of the following letter parts, adding the missing capitals.

EXAMPLE: dear uncle harry,   *Dear Uncle Harry,*

1. dear rabbi hartman, _____
2. your grateful neighbor, _____
3. with deep regret, _____
4. my dear ethel, _____
5. sincerely yours, _____
6. dear chairman gott: _____
7. your friend always, _____
8. dear sir or madam: _____
9. dearest cousin, _____
10. with warm regards, _____

11.2 Abbreviation

Names and Titles of People

Use a person's full given name in formal writing, unless the person uses initials as part of his or her formal name. Abbreviations of titles before and after names begin with capitals and end with periods. Social titles and titles after names are almost always abbreviated, as is *Dr.* before a name. Other titles may be abbreviated if they appear with the full name.

Social Titles	Other Titles	Titles After Names
Mrs. Anderson	Dr. Farway	Alex Dane, Jr.
Messrs. Peters and Hall	Prof. Donna Sample	Roberta Deal, M.D.

Geographical Terms

Abbreviations for geographical terms before or after a proper noun begin with a capital letter and end with a period. Traditional abbreviations for states begin with a capital and end with a period. Postal Service abbreviations are two capitals with no period. None of these abbreviations are used in formal writing.

Geographical Terms	States (Traditional)	States (Postal Service)
Denver Rd.	Mich.	MI
Mt. Whitney	Ore.	OR

EXERCISE A: Using Abbreviations in Formal Writing. On the line at the right of each item, write the correct abbreviation for the underlined word or words. If the abbreviation could be used in formal writing, put a check (√) after it.

EXAMPLE: Mister John D. Barker   *Mr.√*

1. Donna Brock, Doctor of Medicine _____
2. Governor Al Smith _____
3. Sue Ames, Registered Nurse _____
4. Senator Rinaldo _____
5. Professor Wexler _____
6. Washington Square _____
7. Fort Lauderdale _____
8. Park Avenue _____
9. New Haven County _____
10. President Calvin Coolidge _____
11. Apartment 60 _____
12. Arden Pease, Doctor of Divinity _____
13. Ensign Schrier _____
14. Connell Street _____
15. Doctor Rivera _____
16. Private Ruppert Watts _____
17. Admiral Crockett _____
18. Pike's Peak _____
19. Captain Eberhard Watson _____
20. Mount Mansfield _____

EXERCISE B: More Work with Abbreviations. Correctly abbreviate each item.

EXAMPLE: Ambassador   *Amb.*

1. Colorado (traditional) _____
2. New Hampshire (Postal Service) _____
3. Major General _____
4. Boulevard _____
5. Island _____
6. Secretary _____
7. National Park _____
8. Nebraska (Postal Service) _____
9. Wyoming (traditional) _____
10. Block _____

NAME _____ CLASS _____ DATE _____

11.2 Abbreviation

Time, Measurements, and Numbers

Use the examples in the chart below as guidelines for using capitals and periods in time abbreviations. Abbreviations for clocked time, days, and months may not be used in formal writing.

Clocked Time	Days	Months	Before/After Noon	Historical Dates
sec.	Mon.	Jan.	A.M. a.m.	B.C.

For the abbreviations of most traditional measurements use small letters and periods. For most metric measurements use small letters and no periods. Use these abbreviations only with numbers.

Traditional Measurements		Metric Measurements	
pt. pint(s)	F. Fahrenheit	kL kiloliter(s)	C Celsius

In formal writing, spell out numbers or amounts of less than one hundred and any other numbers that can be written in one or two words. Also spell out all numbers found at the beginning of sentences. Use numerals for fractions, decimals, percentages, addresses, and dates.

Numbers as Words	Numerals
seventy-two cupcakes One hundred twenty-three attended.	72 percent of the students We sold 123 tickets.

Latin Expressions

Use small letters and periods for most abbreviations of Latin expressions. Avoid these abbreviations in formal writing.

LATIN EXPRESSIONS	
i.e. (that is)	pro tem. (for the time, temporarily)

EXERCISE A: Working with Abbreviations. Write the correct abbreviation for each item in the left-hand column. Write the meaning for each abbreviation in the right-hand column.

EXAMPLES: seconds __sec.__   i.e. __that is__

1. meter _____
2. inches _____
3. note well _____
4. Fahrenheit _____
5. for example _____
6. pro tem. _____
7. g _____
8. km _____
9. gal. _____
10. C _____

EXERCISE B: Working with Numbers. Complete each item with the correct form of the number given in parentheses.

EXAMPLE: (1,000) __one thousand__ dollars

1. (32) _____ trees
2. (6.5) _____ percent
3. (152) _____ soldiers were injured in the attack.
4. (239) _____ Charter Place
5. (300) _____ copies

Copyright © by Prentice-Hall, Inc.

NAME _____ CLASS _____ DATE _____

11.2 Abbreviation

Business and Government Groups

An abbreviated word in a business name begins wih a capital letter and ends with a period. Use all capitals and no periods to abbreviate names whose abbreviations are pronounced letter by letter as well as for acronyms that form names.

Business Abbreviatons	Letter-by-Letter Names	Acronyms
Bros. Corp. Ltd.	NFL NBC NLRB	NASA OPEC
Co. Inc. Mfg.	AMA VA CPR	NATO DOT

Other Common Abbreviations

Study other commonly used abbreviations until you are familiar with them.

MISCELLANEOUS ABBREVIATIONS	
aux. (auxiliary)	mdse. (merchandise)
fwd. (forward)	vol. (volume)

EXERCISE A: Business and Government Abbreviations. Write an abbreviation or acronym for each item at the left. Write the meaning of each item at the right.

EXAMPLE: Congress of Racial Equality _CORE_   AP _Associated Press_

1. Housing and Urban Development _____
2. Political Action Committee _____
3. Limited _____
4. Columbia Broadcasting System _____
5. Civil Aeronautics Board _____
6. Incorporated _____
7. Individual Retirement Account _____
8. Atomic Energy Commission _____
9. On Job Training _____
10. National Football League _____

11. UMW _____
12. GM _____
13. Corp. _____
14. NATO _____
15. FBI _____
16. IRS _____
17. Co. _____
18. UN _____
19. YMCA _____
20. Bros. _____

EXERCISE B: More Work with Abbreviations. Follow the directions for Exercise A.

EXAMPLES: department _dept._   hi-fi _high fidelity_

1. dozen _____
2. miscellaneous _____
3. volume _____
4. each _____
5. weight _____
6. anonymous _____
7. miles per hour _____
8. approximately _____
9. spelling _____
10. associate _____

11. ill. _____
12. ht. _____
13. hdqrs. _____
14. mtge. _____
15. hosp. _____
16. chap. _____
17. r.p.m. _____
18. govt. _____
19. pg. _____
20. cap. _____

NAME _____ CLASS _____ DATE _____

12.1 End Marks

Basic Uses of End Marks

Use a period to end a declarative sentence, a mild imperative, or an indirect question. Use a question mark to end an interrogative sentence, an incomplete question, or a statement intended as a question. Use an exclamation mark to end an exclamatory sentence, a forceful imperative, or an interjection expressing strong emotion.

Periods	Question Marks	Exclamation Marks
No one answered the door.	Is anyone home?	How long we have waited!
Ring the bell again.	Why not?	Keep knocking!
I wonder where Ed could be.	It doesn't work?	Whew! There's someone coming.

Other Uses of End Marks

Use a period to end most abbreviations and after numbers and letters in outlines. Use a question mark in parentheses after a fact or statistic to show its uncertainty.

Periods	Question Marks
Roger Marple, D.D.S.	The owner offered a $50 (?) reward.
I. The era of live TV	April 15 (?) is Easter this year.
A. The variety show	

EXERCISE A: Using End Marks for Sentences and Phrases. Write the proper end mark at the end of each item.

EXAMPLE: I must have misunderstood. You didn't mean that __?__

1. What a beautiful town that was _____
2. What time does the second feature begin _____
3. The child asked how long his parents would be gone _____
4. That was a first down. Super _____
5. Duck _____
6. I have misplaced my notecards _____
7. How pleased Grandma was to see us _____
8. I wondered how long the test would take _____
9. Check over your work before you hand in your paper _____
10. When did Andy call _____

EXERCISE B: Using End Marks in Your Own Sentences. Follow the directions to write your own sentences.

EXAMPLE: Write a sentence that suggests uncertainty about a date.
    Lincoln was assassinated on April 14, 1865 (?).

1. Write a sentence that contains an abbreviation for a title.

_____

2. Write a sentence that begins with a strong interjection.

_____

3. Write a sentence that expresses uncertainty about a price.

_____

4. Write a sentence that includes an indirect question.

_____

Copyright © by Prentice-Hall, Inc.

12.2 Commas

Commas That Separate Basic Elements

Use a comma before the conjunction to separate two independent clauses in a compound sentence. Use commas to separate three or more words, phrases, or clauses in a series. Use commas to separate coordinate adjectives.

COMMAS THAT SEPARATE BASIC ELEMENTS	
Independent Clauses	Everyone played well, but we still lost the game. Several people were ill, so we postponed the party.
Elements in a Series	Billy, Joe, and Ed tried out for the team. (3 people) Billy Joe and Ed tried out for the team. (2 people)
Adjectives	That ring contains a rare, exotic gem. (coordinate) My grandmother just got a new fur coat. (cumulative)

EXERCISE A: Using Commas Correctly. Add commas where they are needed; not all sentences need commas.

EXAMPLE: The first four batters were Kyle Marc Pete and Jason.
The first four batters were Kyle, Marc, Pete, and Jason.

1. The dessert had a fluffy cream topping.
2. We requested the book weeks ago yet it hasn't come back so far.
3. The cookies should be cooled drizzled with melted chocolate and sprinkled with chopped nuts.
4. The fish was served with a rich tangy sauce.
5. The marshmallows melted in the steaming hot chocolate.
6. Paula tried to reach Jack all day but she had no luck.
7. Potted palms Easter lilies and pink azaleas banked the stage.
8. My first job was a happy rewarding experience.
9. We had hoped to see that new musical but no tickets were available.
10. Mr. Hawkins has a large collection of rare valuable coins.

EXERCISE B: Recognizing Rules for Commas. Describe the comma rule for each sentence in Exercise A by writing *compound sentence*, *series*, *coordinate adjectives*, or *cumulative adjectives*.

EXAMPLE: ____series____

1. _____
2. _____
3. _____
4. _____
5. _____
6. _____
7. _____
8. _____
9. _____
10. _____

NAME _____ CLASS _____ DATE _____

12.2 Commas

Commas That Set Off Added Elements

Use a comma after an introductory word, phrase, or clause. Also use commas to set off a variety of parenthetical expressions and all nonessential expressions.

COMMAS WITH ADDED ELEMENTS	
Introductory Words	*Frankly*, I doubt we will win.
Introductory Phrases	*Not having studied*, I was nervous about the test.
Introductory Clauses	*As soon as the curtain fell*, the audience applauded.
Direct Address	There is no question, *Pam*, that you are right.
Certain Adverbs	We should note, *however*, that membership is rising.
Common Expressions	That watch, *as a matter of fact*, is a family heirloom.
Contrasting Expressions	Please give this note to Ben, *not to his brother*.
Nonessential Expressions	Bonnie, *who is new in town*, comes from San Diego.

EXERCISE A: Using Commas with Added Elements. Add commas where they are needed in these sentences.

EXAMPLE: Luckily the train had not pulled out yet.
Luckily, the train had not pulled out yet.

1. What time is dinner Mom?
2. Before I knew what was happening I was at the bottom of the stairs.
3. I think that in addition we should get a small gift for Mr. Bailey.
4. Without thinking of his own safety the firefighter rushed into the burning building.
5. The principal not the class advisor will make the final decision.
6. Several teachers moreover have given us their support.
7. The previous owner I assure you took excellent care of this car.
8. Don't you think Ellen that we need more punch?
9. Once the movie was over I wondered why I had sat through the whole thing.
10. Tanya is without a doubt a stronger candidate than Mandy.

EXERCISE B: Distinguishing Between Essential and Nonessential Elements. Decide whether the underlined words in each sentence are essential or nonessential. If they are nonessential, add commas where they are needed. If they are essential, make no changes.

EXAMPLE: Their new house, <u>a restored New England farmhouse</u> is charming.
Their new house, <u>a restored New England farmhouse</u>, is charming.

1. Yul Brynner created the role of the king in the musical *The King and I*.
2. The song "Shall We Dance?" comes from *the King and I* <u>which was written by Rodgers and Hammerstein</u>.
3. The woman <u>approaching the podium</u> is the governor-elect.
4. The gloves <u>that I gave Mom</u> were the wrong color.
5. This sweater <u>which was a gift from my aunt</u> was handmade in Scotland.
6. Emily Dickinson <u>who seldom left her home in Amherst</u> became famous only later.
7. The reporter <u>who wrote that story</u> was a classmate of my father's.
8. The President <u>speaking unofficially to reporters</u> deplored the act.
9. Jeremy <u>a somewhat retiring person</u> surprised us all by winning the debate.
10. The famous soprano <u>Beverly Sills</u> will host the benefit.

12.2 Commas

Other Uses of the Comma

When a date, a geographical name, or an address is made up of two or more parts, use a comma after each part. Also use commas in the other situations shown in the chart below.

Date	On Friday, July 8, 1983, Grandma retired.
Geographical Name	We visited Phoenix, Arizona, on our vacation.
Address	The building at 597 Fifth Avenue, New York, New York, may be declared a National Historic Site.
Name with Title	Carol Hartman, LL.D., will give the second speech.
Salutation and Closing	Dear Uncle Jed, Very truly yours,
Large Numbers	2,687 3,489,620
Elliptical Sentence	Pam is going to Purdue next year; John, to Brown.
Direct Quotation	"Our next contestant," said the emcee, "is a banker."
To Avoid Confusion	With Betty, Jean planned the entire party.

EXERCISE A: Adding Commas to Sentences. Insert commas where they are needed.

EXAMPLE: The Hermitage near Nashville Tennessee was Andrew Jackson's home.
                      The Hermitage near Nashville, Tennessee, was Andrew Jackson's home.

1. An article by Janet Coburn M.D. appeared in the Sunday magazine supplement.
2. My favorite breakfast is ham and eggs; Dad's pancakes and sausage.
3. In one week the station attracted 1238 new subscribers.
4. "I wonder" Joyce said "if anyone gave Tim my message."
5. Phil's new address is 17026 Parker Court Dover Delaware 19901.
6. To Peggy Anne confided her deepest fears.
7. On June 20 1986 my sister will graduate from law school.
8. Entry-level salaries at that factory are $14000 a year.
9. "In the south wing" the guide continued "were the family's private living quarters."
10. Besides coffee cake is needed to feed this hungry crew.

EXERCISE B: Punctuating a Letter. Add commas wherever necessary in the following letter.

                        672 Pondfield Road
                        Bronxville New York 10708
                        October 25 1985

Dear Gerri

   Well it looks as if I will see you this fall after all. My family and I will be coming to Bronxville next Saturday November 2 to visit Sarah Lawrence College. It has been a busy fall with all this college shopping going on. My current favorite is Rutgers in New Brunswick New Jersey. In addition we have visited Fairleigh Dickinson St. Johns and Hunter. I am applying to all of them but I haven't made any firm decision yet.

   My parents would like to take us out to lunch when we are in town next Saturday so think of some likely places. It will be good to see you again.

                        Your old friend
                        Sal

NAME _____ CLASS _____ DATE _____

12.3 Semicolons and Colons

The Semicolon

Use semicolons in situations such as those illustrated in this chart.

USES OF THE SEMICOLON	
Independent Clauses Without Coordinating Conjunctions	The walls had been gray; we painted them yellow.
With Conjunctive Adverbs	Jim's chances were poor; nevertheless, he won the marathon.
With Transitional Expressions	Singles tennis games require energy; at the same time, they are fun.
With Elements Already Containing Commas	Our summer house, a ramshackle bungalow, is far from elegant; but the views from the porch are spectacular.

The Colon

Use a colon after an independent clause to introduce the following elements: list of items, a formal quotation, a summarizing or explanatory sentence, and a formal appositive. Also use colons in the other situations shown in the chart.

USES OF THE COLON	
Lists	These students are competing: Ed Barker, Janet Arms, and Phil Mason.
Formal Quotations	The doctor turned to the woman: "There is no hope."
Explanatory Sentences	Our neighbor is wealthy: Her grandmother left her a million dollars.
Formal Appositives	We were lucky to get such a good advisor: Ms. Ward.
Numerals Giving Time	3:15 A.M. 9:27 P.M.
Periodical References	*National Geographic* 37:285 (volume: page)
Biblical References	Exodus 12:43 (chapter: verse)
Subtitles	*Write If You Get Work: The Best of Bob and Ray*
Labels Signaling Important Ideas	Caution: Contents are under pressure; do not use near fire, sparks, or flames.

EXERCISE A: Using Semicolons Correctly. In each sentence below a comma is used in place of a semicolon. Circle the comma to show that a semicolon could or should be used there instead.

EXAMPLE: The weight-reduction program does not use scare tactics⊙ it relies on behavior modification.

1. The yearbook, which should be published by mid-May, is still accepting ads from local merchants, however, we have enough ads to cover expenses.
2. Jed overslept, as a result, he wasn't ready when we called for him.
3. I am considering photography, film making, or figure drawing as an elective, but typing, driving, or career planning seem more practical.
4. Greg plans to follow in his father's footsteps, he is studying law.

EXERCISE B: Using Colons Correctly. Add colons where they are needed.

EXAMPLE: The agent nodded "The 7 55 is boarding on Track 2."
　　　　　　The agent nodded: "The 7:55 is boarding on Track 2."

1. These holiday plants are poisonous holly, mistletoe, and poinsettias.
2. The senator pounded the table "I refuse to concede."
3. The article was in *The New England Journal of Medicine* 11 215.
4. The solution seems plain We must attract more sponsors.

12.4 Quotation Marks and Underlining

Quotation Marks for Direct Quotations

A direct quotation represents a person's exact speech or thoughts and is enclosed in quotation marks (" "). An indirect quotation reports only the general meaning of what a person said or thought and does not require quotation marks. In writing direct quotations, use a comma or colon after an introductory expression and a comma, question mark, or exclamation mark after a quotation followed by a concluding expression. If there is an interrupting expression in the middle of a quoted sentence, set it off with commas. If an interrupting expression falls between two quoted sentences, treat it as a concluding expression.

Direct Quotations	Indirect Quotations
Sue asked, "What can I do to help?" "What can I do to help?" Susan asked.	Sue asked what she could do to help.
"I have a feeling," said Joe, "that a storm is brewing."	Joe had a feeling that a storm was brewing.
"Hurry!" shouted Ben. "The train is about to leave."	Ben shouted that we should hurry because the train was about to leave.

EXERCISE A: Distinguishing Between Direct and Indirect Quotations. Label each sentence below *D* (for direct quotation) or *I* (for indirect quotation).

EXAMPLE: Mr. Dillon suggested, Spend no more than twenty minutes on the short answers so that you will have a half hour left for the essay _____D_____

1. Louise suggested that I try out for the part. _____
2. Frank's parents told him that he would be grounded for a month if his grades didn't get better. _____
3. What time shall I pick you up? Audrey inquired. _____
4. Don is sure that Mr. Hawkins will give him a good reference. _____
5. Get off the bus at Dowling Street, Bill explained, and then walk two blocks south to Market. _____
6. That certainly is an odd color for a house, Pete observed. _____
7. Warren remarked that the harpist had been exceptionally good. _____
8. I asked Jill if I could borrow her notes on Chapter 15. _____
9. Oh, my gosh! Phil exclaimed. That jump was incredible! _____
10. Without a doubt, the owner stated, we will surpass last year's sales. _____

EXERCISE B: Using Quotation Marks Correrctly. In each sentence labeled *D* above, add quotation marks where they are needed. Rewrite below each sentence labeled *I* so that it contains a direct quotation.

EXAMPLE: _Mr. Dillon suggested, "Spend no more than twenty minutes on the short answers so that you will have a half hour left for the essay."_

1. _____
2. _____
3. _____
4. _____
5. _____

12.4 Quotation Marks and Underlining

Other Punctuation Marks with Quotation Marks

Always place a comma or a period inside the final quotation mark. Always place a semicolon or colon outside the final quotation mark. Place a question mark or exclamation mark inside the final quotation mark if the end mark is part of the quotation. If the end mark is not part of the quotation, place a question mark or exclamation mark outside the final quotation mark.

PLACING OTHER PUNCTUATION MARKS	
Commas and Periods	"It seems evident," Dad said, "that we need a new roof."
Colons and Semicolons	Ted observed, "What we really need around here is some organization"; then he proceeded to take charge.
Question Marks and Exclamation marks	Pam asked, "Will the test cover only the first chapter?" Didn't Ms. Yu say, "The test will cover only the first chapter"?

Quotation Marks in Special Situations

Use single quotation marks for a quotation within a quotation. Use three ellipsis marks in a quotation to show that words have been omitted. When writing dialogue, begin a new paragraph with each change of speaker. For quotations longer than a paragraph, put quotation marks at the beginning of each paragraph and at the end of the final paragraph.

SPECIAL SITUATIONS IN QUOTATIONS	
Quotation Within a Quotation	Janice asked, "Wasn't it Patrick Henry who said, 'Give me liberty or give me death'?"
Omitted Words	Kennedy's famous line "Ask not what you can do . . ." is from his inaugural address.
Dialogue	"Have you always been interested in gourmet food?" asked the interviewer. 　"Hardly," the famous chef answered. "Until I was sixteen, I subsisted on the typical American junk food diet. I lived for burgers, fries, and shakes and totally rejected anything green or anything that had lived in the ocean. 　"The summer I was sixteen, I went to Europe with my father, and my life was changed forever!"

EXERCISE A: Punctuating Direct Quotations. Add the missing punctuation marks in each sentence.

EXAMPLE: The teacher asked, Who can tell me who said, Et tu, Brute?
　　　　　　The teacher asked, "Who can tell me who said, 'Et tu, Brute'?"

1. Are you sure you told them, Take Exit 7, not 7A? Jane asked.
2. Max reminded me, The book is due on Thursday; but I still forgot.
3. We all hope, Sally wrote, that you will be back in school soon.
4. Have you seen Sharon since she got her hair cut? Donna asked.
5. Joyce exclaimed, What a glorious sunset that is!
6. Ann said, I am submitting my resignation effective immediately; then she left the meeting.
7. Can't you see, Josh pleaded, that we must act quickly?
8. Agnes asked, Who wrote the poem that begins, Whose woods these are . . . ?
9. Mike announced his plan: I will do the yard work and then use their swimming pool.
10. Wow! Harvey said. We can forget about beating this team.

EXERCISE B: Paragraphing Dialogue. Write a short dialogue between two characters. Include at least one quotation that is over a paragraph long.

12.4 Quotation Marks and Underlining

Underlining and Quotation Marks

Underline the titles of books, full-length plays, movies, series, periodicals, long musical compositions, albums, and works of art. In addition, underline the names of individual land, air, sea, and space craft; foreign words not yet accepted into English; numbers, symbols, letters, and words used to name themselves; and words that you want to stress.

USES OF UNDERLINING	
Titles	**Other Uses**
David Copperfield (novel)	the Orient Express (train)
Our Town (play)	the Oceanic (ship)
Casablanca (movie)	Our guide waved au revoir. (foreign word)
The Waltons (TV series)	A schwa looks like an upside down e.
Cleveland Plain Dealer (newspaper)	What does rococo mean? (word as word)
American Gothic (painting)	Leave your boots outside. (emphasis)

Use quotation marks around the titles of short written works, episodes in a series, songs, and parts of long musical compositions or collections.

USES OF QUOTATION MARKS	
"Winter Dreams" (short story)	"Sounds of Silence" (song)
"The Raven" (poem)	"The Glorious Whitewasher" (chapter)
"Before Breakfast" (one-act play)	

The names of sacred writings and their parts and the titles of government charters, alliances, treaties, acts, statutes, and reports require no marking.

TITLES THAT REQUIRE NO MARKING	
the Koran	the Treaty of Paris
the Pentateuch	the Taft-Hartley Act

EXERCISE A: Using Underlining and Quotation Marks. Add underlining and quotation marks where they are needed in these sentences. Not all sentences will require marking.

EXAMPLE: The Wall Street Journal ran an article entitled Adam's Fall.

The Wall Street Journal ran an article entitled "Adam's Fall."

1. The song Moon River was the theme from the movie Breakfast at Tiffany's.
2. The first book of the Old Testament is Genesis.
3. Many of Amy's a's look like o's.
4. O'Neil's Long Day's Journey into Night is a theatrical tour de force.
5. I must learn to stop misusing the word imply.

EXERCISE B: More Work with Underlining and Quotation Marks. Follow the directions for Exercise A.

1. Lindbergh made his famous trans-Atlantic flight in The Spirit of St. Louis.
2. The Fox and the Grapes may be the most famous fable that Aesop wrote.
3. Many consider the painting Guernica Picasso's chef-d'oeuvre.
4. There are some excellent recipes in the chapter Soups and Stews.
5. The title of the novel The Sound and the Fury is taken from a line in Shakespeare's Macbeth.

12.5 Dashes, Parentheses, and Brackets

Dashes

Use dashes to indicate an abrupt change of thought, a dramatic interrupting idea, or a summary statement. Dashes can also be used to set off a nonessential appositive, modifier, or parenthetical expression when it is long, when it is already punctuated, or when you want to be dramatic.

USES OF THE DASH	
Change of Thought	I'd like to finish—oh, well, I can do that later.
Dramatic Interruption	They arrived—can you believe it?—at exactly the same time.
Summary Statement	Speeches, debates, polls—all are part of election tradition.
Nonessential Element	Dolley Madison's gown—the one she wore at her husband's inauguration—is on display at the Smithsonian.

Parentheses

Use parentheses to set off asides and explanations only when the material is not essential or when it consists of one or more sentences. Also use parentheses to set off numerical explanations such as the dates of a person's birth and death and around numbers and letters marking a series.

USES OF PARENTHESES	
Phrases	Fenwick's first novel (probably his best) has never been reprinted.
Sentences	If we go (Have you received the tickets?), we plan to leave early.
Letters, Numbers, and Dates	The job involves (a) preparing budgets, (b) keeping financial records, and (c) issuing checks. Edgar Allan Poe (1809–1849) achieved fame as a short-story writer, poet, and journalist.

EXERCISE A: Using the Dash. Add dashes where they are needed in the following sentences.

EXAMPLE: I told him he drove me to it that his behavior was inexcusable.
           I told him—he drove me to it—that his behavior was inexcusable.

1. Dolls, toy soldiers, trucks all kinds of toys were heaped under the tree.
2. The key is right now where did I put that key?
3. Fame, fortune, critical acclaim all these were suddenly hers.
4. She told me this is just between us, of course that she regrets her decision.
5. The new stadium it boasts a retractable dome seats fifty thousand.

EXERCISE A: Using Parentheses. Add parentheses wherever they are appropriate.

EXAMPLE: One of the twins I don't remember which wanted to join the circus.
           One of the twins (I don't remember which) wanted to join the circus.

1. The first word of the *Odyssey andra*, meaning "man" suggests the theme of the epic.
2. Elizabeth Cady Stanton 1815–1902 was an early champion.
3. The bactrian camel has two humps, while the Arabian camel also called a *dromedary* has only one.
4. Anything used for money must perform three functions: a it must serve as a freely accepted means of exchange; b it must have value in itself; and c it must permit the accumulation of wealth.
5. Pendleton bought ten shares of General Widget the price was the lowest in years and began to regard himself a capitalist.

12.5 Dashes, Parentheses, and Brackets

Brackets

Use brackets to enclose a word or words inserted in a quotation by a writer who is quoting someone else. Brackets are also used sometimes with *sic* (thus) to show that the author of the quoted material misspelled or mispronouncd a word or phrase.

USES OF BRACKETS	
Inserted	The mayor declared, "They [the reporters] have quoted me out of context."
With *sic*	The closing on the letter was "Yours respectively [sic]."

EXERCISE A: Using Brackets Correctly. Add brackets where they are needed in each of the following sentences.

EXAMPLE: The epigram about weather usually attributed to him Mark Twain was actually written by a newspaper editor in Connecticut.
The epigram about weather usually attributed to him [Mark Twain] was actually written by a newspaper editor in Connecticut.

1. The only American to win the world chess championship Bobby Fischer eventually forfeited the title.
2. As Oscar Wilde observed, "It experience is the name everyone gives to their mistakes."
3. One fact in the paper was footnoted as follows: "Found somewhere in *Encyclopaedia Brittanico* sic."
4. In this novel *Pudd'nhead Wilson*, the main character takes up fingerprinting as a hobby.
5. The actor misquoted slightly: "We are such stuff as dreams are made of sic."

EXERCISE B: Using Dashes, Parentheses, and Brackets. Insert the proper punctuation in each sentence.

EXAMPLE: The bar graph see page 146 shows the relation between imports and exports in 1985.
The bar graph *(*see page 146*)* shows the relation between imports and exports in 1985.

1. The legislature is likely to choose one of the following plans for tax reduction: a a cut of 1 percent in the sales tax; b a cut in income taxes; c a reduction of corporate taxes.
2. Mrs. Malaprop accuses Lydia of being "as headstrong as an allegory sic on the banks of the Nile."
3. The smell of greasepaint, the roar of the crowd Tompkins was turning his back on all that.
4. Mr. Wilkes Wasn't he the man that carved birds? is now working on a replica of a California condor.
5. We will need to oh, here comes my bus, finally.

12.6 Hyphens and Apostrophes

Hyphens

Use a hyphen when writing out numbers from *twenty-one* through *ninety-nine* and with fractions used as adjectives. Also use hyphens with certain prefixes and compound nouns, with compound modifiers (unless they are proper adjectives or contain an adverb ending in *-ly*), and to avoid confusion.

USING HYPHENS		
With Numbers	fifty-two cards	one-third cup
With Prefixes	non-Germanic	ex-governor
With Compound Nouns	son-in-law	good-for-nothing
With Compound Modifiers	an ill-timed comment a first-rate player	North American bird highly recommended movie

At the end of a line, divide words only between syllables. Most words with prefixes and suffixes can be divided between the prefix and root or root and suffix. However, never leave a single letter standing alone. In addition, do not divide proper nouns and proper adjectives, divide hyphenated words only after the hyphen, and do not divide a word that falls at the end of a page.

HYPHENS AT THE ENDS OF LINES				
Correct	con-cern	post-pone	re-mark	ex-husband
Incorrect	conc-ern	e-nough	Den-mark	self-de-feat

EXERCISE A: Using Hyphens. Place hyphens where they are needed. (Not all sentences need hyphens.)

EXAMPLES: At the beginning of the story, Scrooge is a tight fisted employer.
At the beginning of the story, Scrooge is a tight-fisted employer.

1. His great grandfather had been Lincoln's best friend.
2. His round head resembled a jack o'lantern.
3. Out of a possible hundred, Alice got ninety six answers right.
4. The route traced on the map is self explanatory.
5. Mark had always wanted to visit New Orleans for the Mardi Gras festivities.
6. The new law requires children's clothing to be made of fire resistant materials.
7. The driver swerved sharply to avoid a head on collision.
8. I did not remember that this was such a totally impossible task.
9. The five story building will be replaced by a much taller one.
10. Senator elect Robinson personally thanked all of her campaign workers.

EXERCISE B: Hyphenating Words. Rewrite each word below, using a hyphen at any place where the word could be divided at the end of a line of writing.

EXAMPLES: carefully _care-ful-ly_   among _among_

1. misspell _____
2. elbow _____
3. erase _____
4. interfere _____
5. all-important _____
6. length _____
7. Belgium _____
8. disagree _____
9. around _____
10. circumspect _____

12.6 Hyphens and Apostrophes

Apostrophes

The possessives of nouns are formed as shown in the first chart below. The possessives of some pronouns are formed with apostrophes, but the possessives of personal pronouns are not. Apostrophes are also used in contractions and a few special plurals.

POSSESSIVE FORMS OF NOUNS			
Singular Nouns	**Plural Nouns**	**Compound Nouns**	**Joint and Individual Ownership**
a day's work	two days' work	sister-in-law's idea	Ted and Paula's dog (joint)
an actress's role	two actresses' roles	Elizabeth I's crown	Ann's and Jim's answers
a man's opinion	two men's opinions	runner-up's words	(individuals)

POSSESSIVE FORMS OF PRONOUNS		
Indefinite		**Personal**
someone's anyone else's		my, mine, our, ours, your, yours
anybody's each other's		his, her, hers, its, their, theirs

OTHER USES OF APOSTROPHES		
Contractions		**Special Plurals**
aren't we'd o'clock		There are three *h*'s in *Khrushchev*.
won't you'd Class of '86		Your *3*'s look like *?*'s.

EXERCISE A: Writing Possessive Forms. Write the possessive form of each noun or pronoun below.

EXAMPLES: goose   _goose's_   they   _their_

1. dress _____
2. children _____
3. anyone _____
4. boys _____
5. days _____
6. each other _____
7. players _____
8. Smiths _____
9. it _____
10. brother-in-law _____
11. women _____
12. geese _____
13. Andy and Steven (joint) _____
14. minutes _____
15. our _____
16. one another _____
17. Lois _____
18. mice _____
19. motorists _____
20. passer-by _____

EXERCISE B: Using Apostrophes in Other Ways. Add apostrophes where they are needed.

EXAMPLE: Arent the members of the Class of '82 having a reunion?
            Aren't the members of the Class of '82 having a reunion?

1. Richie gets straight *A*s in math.
2. Weve put more water in its tank, but the fish still looks unhappy.
3. You shouldnt use so many *and*s.
4. Heres the package that theyve been waiting for.
5. At five oclock, please stop and sort out whats yours and whats ours.

NAME _____ CLASS _____ DATE _____

13.1 Prewriting

Generating Ideas

To gather ideas for writing topics, scan current periodicals and newspapers for events of interest, and survey your own interests, experiences, and ideas.

TECHNIQUES FOR GENERATING IDEAS	
Interviewing Yourself	Ask yourself questions to discover topics that interest you.
Free Writing	Write for a specified amount of time or number of pages.
Journal Writing	Keep a daily record of your thoughts, feelings, and experiences.
Reading and Saving	Read as much and as often as possible, clipping and saving articles that capture your interest.
Clustering	Think of words associated with a chosen topic.
Brainstorming	Start with an idea and build on it, trying to go in as many directions as possible.
Cueing	Use a variety of devices to stimulate ideas.

Choosing and Narrowing a Topic

Limit the scope of your topic so that it can be covered in a paper of the assigned length.

EXERCISE A: Interviewing Yourself. Answer the questions below to help you generate ideas for potential writing topics.

1. What hobbies interest you? _____
   _____

2. What are your major accomplishments? _____
   _____
   _____

3. What kinds of subjects arouse your curiosity? _____
   _____

4. What are your goals in life? _____
   _____
   _____

5. What are your values? _____
   _____
   _____

EXERCISE B: Free Writing. On separate paper, write for ten minutes, nonstop, on any of the following topics. Don't worry about spelling or punctuation. Just keep writing. Start with general reactions and move to specific ones. Include any sights, sounds, or other details associated with the subject.

　　　　starting a new job　　　　　　accepting criticism
　　　　applying to colleges　　　　　the first snowstorm of the year
　　　　making plans for the future　　the coming of spring
　　　　leaving someone you care for　 falling in love
　　　　facing uncertainty　　　　　　striving to reach a goal
　　　　going on a vacation　　　　　 walking through the forest

Copyright © by Prentice-Hall, Inc.

NAME _____ CLASS _____ DATE _____

13.1 Prewriting

Determining Audience and Purpose
Determine your audience and purpose before you begin writing.

Developing a Main Idea and Support
State your main idea in a topic sentence and list the details that support it.

ORGANIZATION OF SUPPORTING INFORMATION	
Chronological Order	Information arranged in time sequence
Spatial Order	Information arranged according to space relationships
Order of Importance	Information arranged from least to most important, or vice versa
Comparison and Contrast	Information arranged according to similarities and differences between items
Developmental	Information arranged so that one point leads logically to the next

EXERCISE A: Determining Audience and Purpose. Choose one of the five broad topics below. Then complete the work that follows.

            college   politics   literature   music   history

1. Use the clustering technique to narrow the topic you have chosen into one that is narrow enough to be covered in a short paper. Then write the topic. _____

2. Write a possible purpose for your paper. _____

3. Write another possible purpose for your paper. _____

4. Identify a potential audience for the purpose you wrote in #2. _____

5. Identify a potential audience for the purpose you wrote in #3. _____

EXERCISE B: Developing a Topic. Complete the work below to develop your topic from Exercise A.

1. Decide on your main idea. _____

2. Make a list of supporting information. _____

3. Choose a method of organizing the information you wrote in #2. _____

4. Arrange your information according to the method you chose in #3. _____

NAME _____ CLASS _____ DATE _____

13.2 Writing

Writing a First Draft

Translate your prewriting notes into sentences and paragraphs, without worrying about punctuation, spelling, grammar, or perfect sentences. While you are writing, you may want to rework your ideas, change your approach, or even change your entire topic.

SAMPLE ROUGH DRAFT

Many people think that the most important aspect of a college education is that it provides young men and women with opportunity to enter into a wide variety of professions after they graduate, but there is a great deal more to be gained by attending college than merely getting a good job later in life. College allows young men and women to explore a wide variety of fields and to develop new areas of interest. Students learn to question institutions and values that they may have unquestioningly accepted in the past and, by doing so, develop their own sets of values and their own interpretations of the institutions of our society. At the same time, students learn to get along with one another on a day to day basis. Students are forced to learn to respect each other's needs and to learn to adapt to different situations. A spirit also develops among the students through participation in extracurricular activities. This spirit often carries on into later life, as the young men and women develop a strong attachment to their colleges. Overall, college is an extremely valuable and enriching experience.

EXERCISE A: Writing a First Draft. Choose one of the topics below. Then write a paragraph based on the prewriting information that follows. Feel free to rework the ideas that are presented below as you are writing, and do not hesitate to use some of your own ideas to assist you in developing your paragraph.

Topics:	choosing a career	dance fads	why reading is important
Purposes:	to inform	to entertain	to persuade
Audiences:	your classmates	young people	general audience
Order:	developmental	chronological	order of importance
Supporting Information:	1. keep options open 2. survey your interests 3. narrow choices down to several broad fields 4. Explore specific job possibilities in each field	1. variety of dance crazes during 1950's 2. 1960's go-go craze 3. 1970's disco dancing 4. 1980's new wave slam dancing, break dancing	1. helps in development of writing skills 2. allows the discovery of new interests and the exploration of new fields 3. helps encourage people to think 4. important part of a person's overall intellectual development

EXERCISE B: More Work with First Drafts. On separate paper, write a first draft based on the prewriting activities that you completed in Exercise A and B on page 94. Do not worry about grammar, spelling, or punctuation. Just get your thoughts down on paper. Once you have finished, save your paper so that you can work on revising it.

Copyright © by Prentice-Hall, Inc.

NAME _____ CLASS _____ DATE _____

13.3 Revising

Revising for Sense

Make sure that all of the ideas in your paper support your purpose and that you have presented them in a logical manner and have made the connections between them apparent.

REVISING FOR SENSE

1. Make sure that you have clearly stated your topic.
2. Make sure that your main idea will be clear to your readers.
3. Make sure that there is enough relevant supporting information.
4. Make sure that your ideas are presented in a logical order.
5. Make sure that the logical connections between ideas have been expressed.

Editing for Word Choice and Sentence Variety

Read your paper several times, making sure that every word serves your purpose and that your sentences are clear and varied.

EDITING WORDS AND SENTENCES

1. Make sure that each word conveys the meaning that you intended it to.
2. Make sure that the language is appropriate for the intended audience.
3. Make sure that the meaning of each sentence is clear.
4. Make sure that you have varied the lengths and structures of your sentences.

Proofreading and Publishing

Proofreading involves making final corrections in spelling, capitalization, punctuation, and grammar. Once you have your final version, decide on the best way to distribute it to your intended audience.

EXERCISE A: Revising and Editing a Paper. Revise and edit the paper you wrote in Exercise B on page 95 by answering the questions below and by making appropriate changes when your response to a question is *no*.

1. Have you made your topic and main idea clear to your readers? _____
2. Is there enough relevant supporting information and is it presented in a logical manner? _____
3. Does each word in your paper convey the meaning that you intended it to? _____
4. Is the language appropriate for the intended audience and is the meaning of each sentence clear? _____
5. Have you varied the lengths and structures of your sentences? _____

EXERCISE B: Proofreading a Paper. Proofread the paper you revised in Exercise A, correcting any errors in grammar, spelling, punctuation, and capitalization. Then recopy your paper neatly and think of how you want to present it to your audience.

NAME _____ CLASS _____ DATE _____

13.4 Finding Your Own Approach

Adapting the Steps

Experiment with the planning, writing, and revising steps to find a process that works well for you.

POSSIBLE ADAPTATIONS OF THE STEPS
1. Brainstorm for support before you look for a main idea. 2. Write a first draft without preparing an outline. 3. Revise as you write, sentence by sentence.

EXERCISE A: Varying the Prewriting Steps. Think of a specific topic that you could use to write a paragraph. Then complete the activities below.

1. What is your topic? _____
2. Brainstorm for supporting information. _____
   _____
   _____
   _____
   _____
   _____
3. Using your list from #2, think of a possible main idea. _____
   _____
4. Using your list from #2, think of another possible main idea. _____
   _____

EXERCISE B: Varying the Writing and Revising Steps. Using your list of supporting information and one of your main ideas from Exercise A, write the first draft of a paragraph in the space provided below without preparing an outline. Revise your paper as you are writing, and save your paper so that you can critically evaluate it.

NAME _____ CLASS _____ DATE _____

13.4 Finding Your Own Approach

Overcoming Writing Problems

Try different techniques for getting started, overcoming writing blocks, and looking critically at your writing.

OVERCOMING WRITING PROBLEMS		
Getting Started	**Overcoming Blocks**	**Gaining Perspective**
1. Look for ideas in your daily environment. 2. Jot topics down, working as fast as possible. 3. Write sentences about topics, working as fast as possible.	1. Reread your work. 2. Talk about what you have written with someone, and discuss what you might write to follow what you have already written.	1. Put your work aside. 2. Share your writing with others. 3. Find an editor to suggest ways of improving your work.

EXERCISE A: Getting Started. Complete the activities below.

1. Walk around your neighborhood looking for potential writing topics. Then write down two of these topics. _____
_____

2. Find two potential writing topics in a magazine or book. _____

3. Using one of your topics from #1, write down as many smaller topics or related ideas as you can. _____

4. Using one of your topics from #2, write down as many smaller topics or related ideas as you can. _____

EXERCISE B: Gaining Perspective. Go back to the paragraph you wrote in Exercise B on page 97. Complete the activities below.

1. Look over your paragraph and comment on ways in which you could improve it. _____
_____

2. Read your paragraph to two of your friends, have them comment on its strengths and weaknesses, and write down their comments. _____
_____
_____

3. Have someone whose opinions you greatly respect read your paragraph and suggest improvements, and write down the suggestions. _____
_____
_____

4. Using the comments and suggestions in #1, 2, and 3, rework your paper and prepare a final draft on separate paper.

NAME _____ CLASS _____ DATE _____

14.1 Using Words Effectively

Choosing Precise Words

Use action verbs in the active voice and vivid, specific words to express your ideas precisely.

PRECISE LANGUAGE
Vague: The train was delayed by a storm, but it finally arrived at the station.
Vivid: A sleet, hail, and ice storm delayed the Metroliner, but it finally rumbled into Washington's vast Union Station.

Choose words whose connotations suit the tone and level of language of your passages, and replace clichés with fresh, direct words and expressions.

CONNOTATIONS			
Positive Tone:	slender	debate	invest
Neutral Tone:	thin	disagreement	spend
Negative Tone:	emaciated	argument	squander
Formal tone:	gaunt	altercation	disburse
Informal Tone:	skinny	brawl	shell out

EXERCISE A: Using Precise Words. Rewrite each sentence, using more precise language.

EXAMPLE: An old path goes to the lake.
  An unused path, partially covered with underbrush, led to the rocky edge of Lake Louise.

1. Because of a change of plans, our trip to the city is impossible.
   _____

2. The bus to the college was delayed by some kind of trouble.
   _____

3. The restaurant near the lake is ugly and uninteresting.
   _____

4. The audience rose together to applaud the President.
   _____

5. After a great deal of effort, the men reached the top of the mountain.
   _____

EXERCISE B: Choosing the Right Connotation. Fill in each blank with the word in parentheses that has the right connotation for the sentence.

EXAMPLE: The leopard __*crouched*__, ready to pounce. (squatted, cringed, crouched, reclined)

1. The new evidence will undoubtedly _____ Brad's partner. (envelop, incriminate, ensnare, blame)
2. The occupying army tried to avoid _____ attacks by guerrillas. (provoking, inspiring, fomenting, producing)
3. In choosing a winner, the committee tried to be completely _____ (indifferent, impartial, unprejudiced, insipid)
4. If Grandpa had not been so _____, the family would not have survived the Great Depression. (parsimonious, miserly, thrifty, stingy)
5. The nobleman was attended by his personal _____. (menials, drudges, servants, lackeys)

99

14.1 Using Words Effectively

Maintaining an Appropriate Tone

Replace slang, jargon, and foreign terms with precise, understandable language, and replace overly emotional language with reasonable language.

Problems in Tone	Improvements
Euphemism: He got his walking papers.	He was fired.
Self-Important Language: He perceived an opportunity to dine sumptuously at the expense of another.	He saw a chance for a free meal.
Slang: The boss sent her stooge.	The boss sent her subordinate.
Jargon: Our group will interface with yours.	Our group will meet and exchange ideas with yours.
Foreign Term: Let's keep this *entre nous*.	Let's keep this between us.
Overly Emotional Language: This law is another example of blatant disregard for the underdog.	This law does not take into account the well-being of all groups affected by it.

EXERCISE A: Solving Problems in Tone. Rewrite each sentence, eliminating any words that cause problems in tone.

EXAMPLE: Sal was bamboozled by the turn of events.
   Sal was confused by the turn of events.

1. Bobby was hassling Fred this morning.

2. He expressed his hostility by physically abusing his male sibling.

3. She promised to finish her report in a snap.

4. Her disrespectful remark to the minister was a terrible *faux pas*.

5. The manager has a new angle he wants to explore.

EXERCISE B: More Work with Tone. Follow the directions for Exercise A.

1. The prisoner of war was terminated by his captors.

2. Marcia's bellicose statement will be taken as a declaration of war.

3. Ella was freaked out when she learned the news.

4. Two goons guarded the entrance to the building.

5. The legislature hoped to pass the bill *sub rosa*.

NAME _____ CLASS _____ DATE _____

14.1 Using Words Effectively

Using Words Concisely

Make your writing concise by eliminating nonessential words.

Wordy Sentences	Concise Sentences
Empty Words: *It is a fact that* he was President in 1962.	He was President in 1962.
Hedging Words: Bob *sort of* wants to pitch tomorrow.	Bob wants to pitch tomorrow.
Redundancy: *The length of* the hose was five feet long.	The hose was five feet long.

When possible, reduce wordy phrases and clauses to shorter structures.

Wordy Structures	Concise Constructions
We submit this complaint *with all due respect.*	We *respectfully* submit this complaint.
Sally, *who is our captain,* was injured in the game.	Sally, *our captain,* was injured in the game.

EXERCISE A: Eliminating Empty Words, Hedging Words, and Redundancy. Rewrite each sentence to make it more concise.

EXAMPLE: He is of the opinion that the game will be canceled.
  He thinks that the game will be canceled.

1. On Christmas she kind of wished for snow.

2. Bess couldn't take gym due to the fact that she was unprepared.

3. It seems that the state highway was flooded in the storm.

4. His writing was characterized by repetition and redundancy.

5. The new theater is located in the area of the shopping mall.

EXERCISE B: Reducing Wordy Constructions. Rewrite each sentence to make it more concise.

EXAMPLE: For this graphic we need pigments that are unusually bright.
  For this graphic we need unusually bright pigments.

1. The woman who is wearing a red hat is our new mayor.

2. The lawyer chose his words with great care.

3. My father wants a stereo system that is more advanced.

4. Atlanta, which is often called the hub of the South, is a good place to open a business.

5. The students decided to hold a bake sale, and they also decided to have a car wash.

14.2 Using Words in Special Ways

Using Figures of Speech
Use similes to emphasize the shared qualities of otherwise dissimilar items. Use metaphors to heighten an imaginative connection between two items.

FIGURES OF SPEECH
Simile: I wandered *lonely as a cloud*...—Wordsworth *Metaphor:* All the *world's a stage.*—Shakespeare

Setting Moods
Use sensory impressions to recreate particular experiences and help create moods for your audience.

USING SENSORY IMPRESSIONS
A biting wind ripped through our dark camp, stinging our ears and burning our lips. Nearby, a branch crashed suddenly to the ground, and Lisa cried out. Inching closer to the crackling fire, we could smell and almost taste the roasting venison.

Using Professional Models
Study the language used by professional writers in order to improve your own writing style.

EXERCISE A: Writing Similes and Metaphors. Follow the directions for each item below.

EXAMPLE: Write a metaphor about snow.
  Snow blanketed the ground, putting to rest the last of autumn's fallen leaves.

1. Write a simile using *as brittle as* in your comparison.

2. Write a metaphor comparing a person with an animal.

3. Write a simile about physical or inner strength.

4. Write metaphor about a woman's eyes.

5. Write a simile comparing a person with a tree or flower.

EXERCISE B: Using Sensory Impressions. Choose two of the topics listed below. For each topic you choose, write two or three sentences that include a number of different sensory impressions.

    A trip on a motor boat   The beginning of a job interview
    A fabulous dessert   Taking a driver's test

1.

2.

NAME _____ CLASS _____ DATE _____

15.1 Improving Your Sentences

Sentence Combining

Combine short sentences by using compound subjects or verbs; phrases; or compound, complex, or compound-complex sentences.

Separate Sentences	Combined Sentences
Otis is a very talented guitarist. Alice also plays the guitar very well.	Otis and Alice are both very talented guitarists.
He lost control of his car. It spun out and slammed into a tree.	When he lost control of his car, it spun out and slammed into a tree.
The game had ended. Some of the fans moved quickly toward the exits. Others remained in the stands to celebrate their team's victory.	Once the game had ended, some of the fans moved quickly toward the exits while others remained in the stands to celebrate their team's victory.

EXERCISE A: Sentence Combining. Combine the sentences in each item into a single, longer sentence.

EXAMPLE: Chuck received an athletic scholarship. He accepted it gratefully.
When Chuck received an athletic scholarship, he accepted it gratefully.

1. Elizabeth Fox is now a district attorney. She is a former congresswoman. _____

2. Fred is a gifted athlete. He is also a good student. _____

3. Sandy waited in line for eight hours to buy tickets for the concert. All the tickets were sold before she reached the front of the line. _____

4. Ron slipped and fell into a puddle. He ruined his best pair of pants. _____

5. The school's football team won easily. The soccer team was defeated. _____

EXERCISE B: More Work with Combining Sentences. Follow the directions in Exercise A.

1. Violet Snodgrass won the talent competition. She is an excellent actress. _____

2. Tim raced through the airport. He was trying to locate the gate his parents would be coming through. _____

3. Mr. and Mrs. Franklin returned from their vacation. They discovered that their house had been broken into. Nothing valuable had been stolen. _____

4. The wind whistled through the trees. The sound of thunder echoed through the air. The rain steadily pounded the ground. _____

5. School was canceled for the day. There had been a major snowstorm the previous night. Most of the students spent the day playing in the snow. _____

NAME _____ CLASS _____ DATE _____

15.1 Improving Your Sentences

Expanding Short Sentences

Eliminate short, choppy sentences by adding details or combining ideas.

Short Sentences	Expanded Sentences
Frank walked down the street.	Frank walked at an accelerated pace down the dark, deserted city street.
The skydiver jumped out of the plane.	Without hesitating to look down at the ground hundreds of feet below, the skydiver jumped out of the plane.

Shortening Long Sentences

Eliminate long, rambling sentences by regrouping ideas into two or more simpler sentences.

Long, Complicated Sentence	Shorter, Clearer Sentences
Almanacs, which dealt at first only with agricultural affairs, attracted interest early in the Colonial Period and really became an institution with the publication of Benjamin Franklin's *Poor Richard's Almanac* in the Revolutionary Period.	Almanacs, which dealt at first only with agricultural affairs, attracted interest early in the Colonial Period. They really became an institution with the publication of Benjamin Franklin's *Poor Richard's Almanac* in the Revolutionary Period.

EXERCISE A: Expanding Short Sentences. Improve each of the sentences by adding details.

EXAMPLE: The team won the game.
The visiting team won the game decisively.

1. Todd's research paper had many faults.

2. The business district is congested.

3. Men are repairing the main highway.

4. Fran drove through the snowstorm.

5. Dave and Bridget watched the sunset.

EXERCISE B: Shortening Long Sentences. Divide each long sentence into two or more sentences.

1. Colorado, a state which produces sugar beets and potatoes as well as coal and silver, really boomed with the discovery of gold in 1859 although it wasn't admitted to the union as the thirty-eighth state until 1876.

2. For the annual spring picnic, the senior class voted to have a barbecue at Closter Lake, where there are facilities for swimming, a softball field, and a volleyball court, and a committee was formed to organize the event, but no one could agree on a date for the picnic.

15.1 Improving Your Sentences

Using Different Sentence Openers and Structures
Avoid monotony in your writing by varying sentence openers and sentence structure.

DIFFERENT SENTENCE OPENERS
Adjectives: Tired and depressed, she burst into tears. *Participial Phrase:* Crossing the finish line, he raised his arms. *Infinitive Phrase:* To find a route, she consulted a map. *Adverb Clause:* Since they left, nothing is the same. *Subject/Appositive:* Mrs. Greene, our counselor, led the discussion. *Transitional Phrase:* For that reason, we decided to stay. *Inverted Order:* Around and around whirled the dancers.
DIFFERENT SENTENCE STRUCTURES
Simple: The game was canceled. *Compound:* The game was canceled, so we went to the movies. *Complex:* Since the game was canceled, we went to the movies. *Compound-Complex:* When the game was canceled, we went to the movies, but we did not enjoy the show.

EXERCISE A: Writing Sentences with Different Openers. Rewrite each sentence below so that it begins with the construction given in parentheses.

EXAMPLE: Bob left the office; he was finished for the day. (participial phrase)
   Finished for the day, Bob left the office.

1. Marni checked the telephone directory to get the number. (infinitive phrase)

2. My new tape deck is an Aiwa and it has Dolby B and C. (appositive)

3. The committee approved the plan although I disagreed. (adverb clause)

4. Mary accepted the award; she was smiling happily. (participial phrase)

5. The weary hikers trudged up the hill. (inverted order)

EXERCISE B: Varying Sentence Structure. Rewrite each set of simple sentences below to create the sentence structure given in parentheses.

EXAMPLE: Joey tied the boat to the dock. Anna cleaned the fish. (complex)
   While Joey tied the boat to the dock, Anna cleaned the fish.

1. The crowd was small. It inspired the team. (complex)

2. We knocked several times. No one answered. (compound)

3. I'm baby-sitting for Emma. She is a charming child. We have fun together. (compound-complex)

4. Meet me at my locker. We can walk home together. (complex)

15.2 Creating Special Effects

Using Different Types of Sentences
Consider using different types of sentences to achieve special kinds of emphasis for your ideas.

DIFFERENT SENTENCE TYPES		
Type	**Characteristics**	**Example**
loose	main idea is presented at the beginning; follows the regular subject-verb-complement order	The manager *explained* the proposal to his staff.
periodic	main idea is presented at the end	After an unusual two hour delay, the *train finally arrived*.
balanced	main ideas are presented in parallel phrases or clauses	*Our first option is to begin* building at once; *our second option is to wait* for an additional loan.
cumulative	main idea is surrounded by layers of detail	*If the senator decides to run again*, he will be elected with one of the largest pluralities on record.

EXERCISE A: Identifying Different Types of Sentences. Label each sentence below *L* for loose, *P* for periodic, *B* for balanced and *C* for cumulative.

EXAMPLE: Early the next morning the rescue began.   *P*

1. Foreign cars get better mileage, but American cars ride better. ____
2. When the votes were tabulated, Mrs. Lester was elected with a higher total number of votes than her managers expected. ____
3. My parents intend to visit Central America next summer. ____
4. At the height of his power and popularity, he resigned. ____
5. I shower in the morning; my sister showers at night. ____

EXERCISE B: Writing Different Types of Sentences. Follow the directions below.

1. Write a loose sentence.

2. Write a periodic sentence.

3. Write a balanced sentence. Punctuate it with a comma and a coordinating conjunction.

4. Write a balanced sentence. Punctuate it with a semicolon.

5. Write a cumulative sentence.

15.2 Creating Special Effects

Using Different Sentence Patterns

Use parallel structures within a sentence and in groups of sentences to point out relationships among ideas.

> **PARALLEL STRUCTURES WITHIN A SENTENCE**
>
> The dramatist agreed *to write a one-act play, to help select the performers,* and *to arrange for production in a local theater.*

Use a contrasting structure to emphasize an idea or to present a concluding thought.

> **CONTRASTING STRUCTURE WITHIN A SENTENCE**
>
> Unable to get support of the media, abandoned by local politicos, and thwarted by the state legislature, *the governor resigned.*

Using Professional Models

Examine and learn from the kinds of sentences that professional writers use.

EXERCISE A: Writing Sentences with Parallel Structures. Follow the directions below.

EXAMPLE: Write a sentence with three parallel verbs.
After breakfast she cleaned the house, did some local shopping, and hopped on a bus to the library.

1. Write a sentence that ends with three prepositional phrases. _____

2. Write a sentence with three or four parallel verbs. _____

3. Write a sentence that begins with two participial phrases connected by *and*. _____

4. Write a sentence that ends with three infinitive phrases. _____

5. Write a sentence with two parallel adverb clauses. _____

EXERCISE B: Writing a Paragraph with a Contrasting Structure. Write a paragraph describing a recent news event. Begin with three to five sentences of normal word length. Then conclude with a brief sentence of no more than four words.

_____
_____
_____
_____
_____
_____

16.1 Connecting Ideas Clearly

Using Transitions

Use transitions to establish relationships among ideas and to clarify the order of ideas.

TRANSITIONS AND THEIR PURPOSES			
To Show Time and Spatial Relationship		**To Show Comparison or Contrast**	**To Show Cause and Effect**
first outside		however	therefore
next near		similarly	consequently
soon before		instead	as a result
finally here		on the other hand	because of
then above			thus
To Show Addition of Ideas		**To Show Emphasis**	**To Show Examples**
also besides		indeed in fact	for instance
too moreover		even especially	for example
first in addition			in particular

EXERCISE A: Choosing Transitions for Sentences. Rewrite each of the following pairs of sentences, adding a transition that best expresses the relationship given in parentheses.

EXAMPLE: We have to clear the underbrush. We have to rake the leaves.   (time)
   We have to clear the underbrush. Then, we have to rake the leaves.

1. I called repeatedly for an interview. I heard from the office manager.   (time)

2. My sister still keeps to a diet of salads. She likes cottage cheese and fresh fruits.   (addition of ideas)

3. The prime minister rejected the proposal. He refused to consider it seriously at all.   (emphasis)

4. My parents first intended to leave this morning. They decided to wait until the storm abated.   (time)

EXERCISE B: Using Transitions to Show Relationships. Write two sentences for each item. Begin the second sentence with a transitional word or phrase from the group indicated.

EXAMPLE: (addition of ideas)   *She was fired for incompetence. Also, she was often ill and frequently late.*

1. (example) _____

2. (time) _____

3. (emphasis) _____

4. (comparison or contrast) _____

108   Copyright © by Prentice-Hall, Inc.

NAME _____ CLASS _____ DATE _____

16.1 Connecting Ideas Clearly

Using Coordination and Subordination

Use coordination and subordination to connect related ideas within sentences. Use coordinating words to join equal, related ideas in a compound sentence. Use subordinating words to join ideas in a complex sentence and to clarify the relationships between ideas of unequal importance.

Coordination	Subordination
Betty expects to give her speech tomorrow, *but* she is prepared to give it today.	*Since* the weather forecast is ominous, we have decided to postpone our trip for at least a week.

EXERCISE A: Using Coordination. Rewrite each of the following pairs of sentences, using an appropriate coordinating word to combine the sentences.

EXAMPLE: I will finish reading *Ironweed* today. I will also work on my research paper.
    I will finish reading Ironweed today, and I will also work on my research paper.

1. I don't agree with Bob's arguments. I can understand his feelings.

2. Susan read the contract carefully. She agreed to sign.

3. Both of us plan to visit colleges during Christmas. We may wait for the winter recess.

4. *On the Waterfront* is a powerful drama. I still prefer *Zorba the Greek*.

5. Snow should begin this evening. It could be a major storm.

EXERCISE B: Using Subordination. Rewrite each of the following pairs of sentences, using an appropriate subordinating word to combine the sentences.

EXAMPLE: The negotiators dislike each other. They will work together.
    Although the negotiators dislike each other, they will work together.

1. The governor decides not to run. The comptroller will run in his place.

2. We expect to tell them the good news. They come home today.

3. Jeff volunteered for the committee. He hopes to be more active this year.

4. Our crop yield was quite poor this year. We will use different fertilizer next time.

5. She returned from Lisbon a week ago. She has been a different person.

Copyright © by Prentice-Hall, Inc.

16.1 Connecting Ideas Clearly

Using Logical Order

Whenever possible, use a logical order to make a series of ideas easier to follow.

Pattern	Explanation
Chronological	Developing a time sequence, generally from an earlier to a later period
Spatial	Describing from left to right, top to bottom, and so on
Order of Importance	Moving from the least important idea to the most important or vice versa

EXERCISE A: Establishing Logical Patterns. Rewrite each group of sentences so that it conforms to a logical pattern. You may change some of the words. Begin by naming the pattern you will use.

EXAMPLE: Cars zoomed past us on the left and the right. We cautiously inched onto the super highway. I noticed the look of panic on the new driver's face.
  Pattern: chronological We cautiously inched onto the super highway. Cars zoomed past us on the left and the right. I noticed the look of panic on the new driver's face.

1. Books lined the walls of the hunter's study. However, the most prominent item in the room was an enormous stuffed moose. Comfortable chairs were arranged around a fireplace. The floors were covered by plush oriental rugs.

   Pattern: _____

2. It was a sunny but cold day when we set out on our camping trip. In late afternoon we reached the campsite, set up our tents, and gathered wood for a fire. As we hiked briskly along, we anticipated a pleasant evening telling stories around a campfire. Then we began to ask one another, "Do you have the matches?"

   Pattern: _____

3. The four-lane highway was completely blocked by the accident. A jackknifed tractor trailer occupied the two center lanes. On the left a panel truck had struck a divider. Victims and spectators milled about. On the right three passenger cars were tangled in a twisted mess.

   Pattern: _____

EXERCISE B: Writing Sentences in Logical Order. Follow the directions below.

1. Write three to four sentences about a view you like. Use spatial order.

2. Write three to four sentences about your goals for the next five years. Use order of importance.

NAME _____ CLASS _____ DATE _____

16.2 Avoiding Problems in Logic

Understanding the Direction of Your Thoughts

In writing, three patterns of reasoning will often provide a logical framework for your ideas: *induction*, *deduction*, and *cause and effect*.

Pattern	Explanation
Induction	Specific information leads to a general conclusion.
Deduction	A general truth leads to one or more specific examples of that truth.
Cause and Effect	One condition causes another to happen.

EXERCISE A: Using Induction and Deduction. Choose one of the following general statements. Circle your choice and then complete the steps below.

General Statements: A college education is not for everyone.
   Good friendships need to be handled with care.
   There are advantages and disadvantages to owning a car.

1. List at least four ideas that support the statement you chose. _____
   _____
   _____

2. Decide whether to use induction or deduction to present your ideas. _____

3. Write a short paragraph presenting your ideas and the general statement. Follow the order you have chosen.
   _____
   _____
   _____
   _____
   _____

EXERCISE B: Using Cause and Effect. Choose one of the following statements, filling in the blank if you choose the first or last. Then complete the steps below.

Statements: The best pets are _____.
   All good athletes have certain characteristics.
   The most important invention of the 20th century is _____.

1. List at least four ideas that support the statement you chose. _____
   _____
   _____

2. Write a short paragraph presenting your ideas and the statement itself. Make any cause-and-effect relationships especially clear.
   _____
   _____
   _____
   _____
   _____

Copyright © by Prentice-Hall, Inc.

NAME _____ CLASS _____ DATE _____

16.2 Avoiding Problems in Logic

Identifying Errors in Logic

In organizing your thoughts, avoid *contradictions, false assumptions, hasty generalizations, non sequiturs,* and statements *begging the question.*

Illogical Support	Definition
Contradiction	An assertion or observation that makes some other statement questionable
False Assumption	A gap in the development of ideas leading to confusion or an incorrect conclusion
Hasty Generalization	An idea presented without sufficient information or reasoning to support it
Non Sequitur	An idea that does not follow logically from the preceding facts or ideas
Begging the Question	An argument that goes in circles by restating ideas where new ideas are promised

Using Professional Models

Study the specific ways professional writers use logical thinking to find models for your own writing.

EXERCISE A: Identifying Illogical Support. In the space provided, indicate the type of illogical support illustrated in each item.

EXAMPLE: Spelling correctly is a problem because it is difficult to do.   *begging the question*

1. Ottawa, the capital of Canada, offers visitors many interesting sights: Parliament, the Parliament library, the Rideau Canal, the war museum, and the National Arts Center. Paris is the capital of France. _____

2. Foreign cars get better mileage because they use less gas.
   _____

3. Everyone agrees that television is worthless. All that it presents is a collection of sitcoms, old movies, and tired quiz shows. _____

4. It is often said that older people tend to have memory lapses. We were not surprised, therefore, when John brought a date to the anniversary party.
   _____

5. Our congressman opposed the new welfare package since most of the people in Congress are opposed to welfare. _____

EXERCISE B: Revising Illogical Support. Rewrite each of the items above, eliminating the illogical support. You may change as many words as necessary to restructure the ideas.

1. _____
   _____
2. _____
   _____
3. _____
   _____
4. _____
   _____
5. _____
   _____

NAME _____ CLASS _____ DATE _____

17.1 Understanding Paragraphs

Topic Sentences
Recognize topic sentences that are too general or too narrow, and revise them to suit the supporting information.

PROBLEMS TO AVOID WITH TOPIC SENTENCES	
Too General	Make sure the topic sentence does not cover more than the rest of the paragraph does.
Too Narrow	Make sure the topic sentence is broad enough to cover all the information in the paragraph.

Support
Supporting information should consist of specific examples, details, facts, reasons, or incidents. Recognize and revise inadequate or inappropriate support.

PROBLEMS TO AVOID WITH SUPPORTING INFORMATION	
Inadequate	Make sure you offer enough supporting information to satisfy your readers.
Inappropriate	Avoid vague statements, generalizations, and weak opinions.

EXERCISE A: Analyzing Topic Sentences. Read the paragraph and then answer the questions that follow it.

(1) Although Amelia Earhart disappeared almost fifty years ago on a flight across the Pacific, her legend continues and experts still speculate about her eventual fate. (2) Born in Atchison, Kansas, in 1898, she early developed an interest in aviation. (3) On June 17, 1928, two men and she flew from Newfoundland to Wales in twenty-one hours in a Fokker flying boat. (4) As a result of this flight, she became an immediate celebrity. (5) In 1937, she and a companion, Fred Noonan, embarked on a 27,000 mile flight around the world. (6) After completing part of her journey, she and Noonan disappeared in the vicinity of the Marshall Islands. (7) No one really knows what happened. (8) One rumor is that she and her companion were captured by Japanese, interrogated for spying on Japanese installations, and executed. (9) There is, however, no doubt that her exploits will continue to live in the annals of aviation history.

1. What is the number of the topic sentence? _____
2. What is wrong with these substitute topic sentences?
   a. Amelia Earhart disappeared on a flight across the Pacific. _____
   b. Amelia Earhart's death is a mystery. _____
   c. Amelia Earhart was a very famous woman. _____
   d. The lives of early pilots were often exciting. _____

EXERCISE B: Analyzing Support. Answer the following questions about the paragraph in Exercise A.
1. What is the main kind of support offered? _____
2. What is the number of a supporting sentence that could be removed without making the support inadequate? _____
3. Which of the following pieces of support would be inappropriate? _____
   a. Like all early pilots, Earhart took unnecessary risks.
   b. It is possible that she and Noonan crashed and died.

Copyright © by Prentice-Hall, Inc.

17.1 Understanding Paragraphs

Unity
A unified paragraph includes only information relevant to the main idea and uses words that are consistent in tone.

Coherence
In a coherent paragraph, the topic sentence and all supporting ideas must follow a logical order, and transitions and other connecting devices should be used to clarify the relationship among the ideas.

USEFUL CONNECTING DEVICES	
Transitions (however, then)	Parallelism
Repeated Main Words and Synonyms	Bridge Ideas
Consistent Pronouns	Concluding Sentences

EXERCISE A: Organizing a Unified Paragraph. Read the randomly organized sentences below. Then answer the questions that follow.

(1) Plastics used in industry are substances made up of organic compounds.
(2) The plastic industry today is growing in an almost nonstop fashion.
(3) Thermosetting plastics, such as Bakelite, are hardened by heat and cannot be softened again.
(4) The plastic cover of a turntable cracked within a year.
(5) The two major types are thermosetting plastics and thermoplastics.
(6) Thermoplastics, such as Lucite, can be softened by heat, shaped, and then rehardened by cooling.
(7) Plastic and wood products have different chemical compositions and uses.
(8) They are derived from synthetic chemicals or natural raw materials.
(9) One or both are used to make lenses, bottles, wire insulation, unbreakable dishes, and storage and trash bags.
(10) As techniques for producing new plastics develop, the future of this industry seems limitless.

1. Which two sentences would you eliminate? ____ ____
2. Which sentence would you choose for the topic sentence? ____
3. Which one would you use as a concluding sentence? ____
4. In what order would you assemble the other six sentences? ____ ____ ____ ____ ____ ____

EXERCISE B: Writing a Coherent Paragraph. Now write the paragraph as you organized it above. Add any transitions or other connecting devices that you think appropriate.

_____
_____
_____
_____
_____
_____
_____
_____

17.1 Understanding Paragraphs

Paragraphs with Special Purposes

Special paragraphs vary in structure from standard paragraphs, but they still help unify the central idea in a longer composition.

PARAGRAPHS WITH SPECIAL PURPOSES	
Introductory Paragraphs	Reveal the topic in an interesting way, often ending with the main point to be covered in the work
Concluding Paragraphs	Touch on earlier ideas and bring the work to a satisfactory end
Continuing Paragraphs	Add more support to the topic sentence in the previous paragraph
Transitional Paragraphs	Act as a bridge between the other paragraphs

EXERCISE A: Writing an Introductory Paragraph. Choose a large topic with which you are familiar and complete the steps below.

1. Topic _____
2. Main point _____
3. Interesting ideas you could use to introduce the main point _____
   _____
4. Introductory paragraph _____
   _____
   _____
   _____
   _____
   _____
   _____
   _____

EXERCISE B: Writing a Concluding Paragraph. Using the material you prepared for Exercise A, write a concluding paragraph for the same longer work. Refer to the main point and end in an interesting, satisfactory way.

_____
_____
_____
_____
_____
_____
_____
_____
_____

Copyright © by Prentice-Hall, Inc.

NAME _____ CLASS _____ DATE _____

17.2 Writing a Paragraph

Prewriting

1. Write your topic below. It should be narrow enough for a single paragraph.

TOPIC: _____

2. Identify the audience for which you will be writing.

AUDIENCE: _____

3. Indicate your purpose (to inform, describe, narrate, or persuade).

PURPOSE: _____

4. Write your main idea. What will the audience learn about the topic?

MAIN IDEA: _____

5. Develop and write an effective topic sentence.

TOPIC SENTENCE: _____

6. Brainstorm and list your supporting information on a separate piece of paper.
7. Choose and list an order for your paragraph (chronological, spatial, order of importance, developmental, and so on).

ORDER: _____

8. Outline your paragraph on a separate piece of paper. Begin with your topic sentence and list your supporting information in the order you have chosen.

Writing

Using your outline, write your paragraph. Choose your words carefully and try to vary your sentence structure. Use several transitional words or phrases to insure coherence.

Revising

Write *yes* or *no* to each of the following questions. Then rework your first draft to improve all the items marked *no*.

1. Is the topic sentence well-phrased and does it contain a main idea that is neither too general nor too narrow? _____
2. Does your topic sentence suggest your purpose and suit your intended audience? _____
3. Does the supporting information contain enough good examples, details, facts, reasons, and so on to develop the topic sentence adequately? _____
4. Does every piece of information belong in the paragraph? _____
5. Is the supporting information arranged in the most logical order? _____
6. Have you achieved coherence by using transitions, coordinating or subordinating words, repetitions of main words, synonyms, and consistent pronouns to connect main ideas? _____
7. Are the word choices the best you can find for your ideas? _____
8. Are your sentences varied in length and structure? _____
9. Is there a good concluding sentence or a generally satisfactory ending? _____
10. Have you corrected all errors in grammar, mechanics, or spelling? _____

After revising your paragraph, **proofread** it carefully and prepare an error-free final copy.

NAME _____ CLASS _____ DATE _____

18.1 Expository and Persuasive Writing

Expository Writing

Expository writing is explanatory and informative.

> **SUGGESTIONS FOR WRITING EXPOSITORY PARAGRAPHS**
>
> 1. Choose a topic that lends itself to factual treatment and that you can write about with authority.
> 2. Determine your audience and its knowledge of the topic.
> 3. Write a factual statement expressing your main idea about your topic.
> 4. Gather supporting information and organize it logically.
> 5. Concentrate on explaining your purpose as you write.
> 6. Revise for unity and coherence.

EXERCISE A: Planning an Expository Paragraph. Circle one of the topics below. Then complete the prewriting activities that follow.

　　　How a piston engine works　　Acting in a school play　　Understanding computers
　　　How to play the piano　　　　How to hit a baseball　　　Planning a budget

1. Identify your audience. _____
2. Decide on a secondary purpose for your paragraph. _____
   _____
3. Write a topic sentence. _____
   _____
4. Write three supporting ideas. _____
   _____
   _____
5. Tell what order you will use. _____

EXERCISE B: Writing an Expository Paragraph. Write an expository paragraph based on the prewriting activities you completed in Exercise A. Use the space provided below.

_____
_____
_____
_____
_____
_____
_____
_____
_____
_____
_____
_____
_____
_____
_____
_____
_____

NAME _____ CLASS _____ DATE _____

18.1 Expository and Persuasive Writing

Persuasive Writing

The main features of persuasive writing are a persuasive purpose and a reasonable, convincing tone.

SUGGESTIONS FOR WRITING A PERSUASIVE PARAGRAPH

1. Choose an issue you care about, and determine whether you can support your opinion about it.
2. Decide on the urgency of your purpose and your tone.
3. Determine your audience and its probable response to your opinion.
4. Express your opinion in a topic sentence and assemble strong supporting arguments. Also, consider the opposition and list evidence for and against your view.
5. Organize your support logically.

EXERCISE A: Planning a Persuasive Paragraph. Circle one of the topics below. Then complete the prewriting activities that follow.

Living in a rural area	Pollution	Illegal aliens
Mandatory gym classes	Violence in professional sports	Plagiarism

1. Identify your audience. _____
2. Write a topic sentence. _____

3. Write two objections that might be raised by people who disagree with you. _____

4. List three arguments you will use in your paper. _____

5. Tell the order you will use. _____

EXERCISE B: Writing a Persuasive Paragraph. Write a persuasive paragraph based on the prewriting activities you completed in Exercise A. Use the space provided below.

NAME _____ CLASS _____ DATE _____

18.2 Descriptive and Narrative Writing

Descriptive Writing

Descriptive writing communicates a dominant impression using language which appeals to the reader's senses, imagination, and emotions.

SUGGESTIONS FOR WRITING DESCRIPTIVE PARAGRAPHS

1. Choose a particular person, object, place, or experience as your topic.
2. Decide on a dominant impression and state it in a topic sentence.
3. List details, sensory impressions, and comparisons that you can use to help establish your dominant impression.
4. Organize your support logically.

EXERCISE A: Planning a Descriptive Paragraph. Circle one of the topics below. Then complete the prewriting activities that follow.

> Skiing in deep powder   Bodysurfing   A deserted alley
> A noisy classroom   An empty church   An elderly man

1. Identify your audience. _____
2. Write a topic sentence. _____
   _____
3. List three specific details. _____
   _____
   _____
4. List two sensory impressions and one figure of speech that you will use. _____
   _____
   _____
5. Tell what order you will use. _____

EXERCISE B: Writing a Descriptive Paragraph. Write a descriptive paragraph based on the prewriting activities you completed in Exercise A. Use the space provided below.

NAME _____ CLASS _____ DATE _____

18.2 Descriptive and Narrative Writing

Narrative Writing

Narrative writing tells a series of related events in a story form, using graphic language.

SUGGESTIONS FOR WRITING NARRATIVE PARAGRAPHS

1. Choose an idea or experience that you can develop into a one-paragraph story.
2. Determine the point of view you will use by considering the different narrators you could have.
3. Write a topic sentence that states a general truth about the experience or simply helps start the action.
4. List the events you will include, organizing them in clear chronological order.

EXERCISE A: Planning a Narrative Paragraph. Circle one of the topics below. Then complete the prewriting activities that follow.

    Moving to a new place   A bitter disappointment   A first date
    Gaining a new friend   Winning an important game   Graduating from school

1. Identify your audience. _____
2. Tell what point of view you will use. _____
   _____
3. Write a topic sentence. _____
4. List three events you will include. _____
   _____
   _____
   _____

5. List three details or impressions that you will use. _____
   _____
   _____

EXERCISE B: Writing a Narrative Paragraph. Use the prewriting activities you completed in Exercise A to write a narrative paragraph. Use the space provided below.

_____
_____
_____
_____
_____
_____
_____
_____
_____
_____
_____
_____

NAME _____ CLASS _____ DATE _____

19.1 Understanding Essays

The Parts of an Essay

A standard essay has a number of structural features, each of which has a particular function.

FEATURES OF STANDARD ESSAYS	
Title	Reflects the main point and purpose and captures the reader's interest
Introduction	Establishes the tone and presents and focuses in on the thesis statement
Body	Presents support for main point in two or more paragraphs, organized by subtopic
Conclusion	Refers to the main point and brings the essay to a satisfactory end

Unity and Coherence in Essays

An essay has unity if each paragraph is unified and if all the paragraphs support and relate to the thesis statement and to each other. An essay has coherence if the ideas within each paragraph and within the essay as a whole are in a logical order and are smoothly connected.

EXERCISE A: Examining an Essay. Find an essay of four to six paragraphs in a magazine or anthology. Use it to complete the following items.

1. What is the title? _____
2. Write a good alternate title. _____
3. What ideas are mentioned in the introduction? (Circle the most interesting.)
   _____
   _____
4. What is the main point? _____
5. Write your own thesis statement to express this point. _____
   _____

EXERCISE B: Looking at Unity and Coherence. Use the essay you selected in Exercise A to complete the following items.

1. How many body paragraphs are there? _____
2. What main idea is developed in each body paragraph?
   (a) _____ (b) _____
   (c) _____ (d) _____
3. In what order are the body paragraphs presented? _____
4. Does the conclusion refer back to the main point, and if so, how?
   _____

5. What other ideas are presented in the conclusion? (Circle the most interesting.)
   _____
   _____

Copyright © by Prentice-Hall, Inc.

19.2 Writing an Essay

Prewriting

1. Choose a suitable topic and write it below.

   TOPIC: _____

2. Identify your audience, making up one if necessary.

   AUDIENCE: _____

3. State your purpose (to inform, persuade, describe, and so on).

   PURPOSE: _____

4. Clearly indicate the main point of your essay.

   MAIN POINT: _____

5. Write your thesis statement. Make certain it is clear, relatively narrow, and capable of being developed in your essay.

   THESIS STATEMENT: _____

6. On a separate sheet of paper brainstorm for support. Think of what the audience needs to know.
7. Decide on your subtopics.

   SUBTOPICS: _____

8. Decide on an order for your subtopics.

   ORDER: _____

9. Outline the body of your essay on a separate sheet of paper.
10. Jot down ideas for the title, introduction, and conclusion.

Writing

Using your outline, complete a rough draft. Keep your audience in mind as you write. Choose your words carefully, try to vary sentence structure, and try to include transitions where they are necessary.

Revising

Write *yes* or *no* to each of the following questions. Then rework your rough draft to improve all the items marked *no*.

1. Is the title appealing and appropriate? _____
2. Does the introduction arouse interest, provide background information, set a tone, and lead toward a main point? _____
3. Is the main point clearly stated in the thesis statement? _____
4. Do the body paragraphs support and develop the subtopics of the thesis statement? Is the main idea of each paragraph clear? _____
5. Have you included enough supporting information—examples, details, facts, reasons, or incidents—to develop each subtopic thoroughly? _____
6. Are the subtopics arranged in logical order? _____
7. Is the information within each paragraph arranged logically and connected with adequate transitions? _____
8. Does the conclusion refer to the main point and complete the essay? _____
9. Have you used the best words you can find to express your ideas? _____
10. Are all your sentences grammatically correct? Have you varied the sentence structure sufficiently? _____

After revising your essay, **proofread** it carefully and prepare an error-free final copy.

NAME _____ CLASS _____ DATE _____

19.3 Writing an Expository Essay

Prewriting

1. Write a suitable topic on the line below.

   TOPIC: _____

2. Identify your audience, making one up if necessary.

   AUDIENCE: _____

3. Now state your purpose (to report, explain, instruct, or define).

   PURPOSE: _____

4. Next write the main point you want to make in your essay.

   MAIN POINT: _____

5. Next write your thesis statement, making sure that it expresses a fact and not an opinion. Try a few out before writing below.

   THESIS STATEMENT: _____

6. On a separate piece of paper, brainstorm for support, keeping your audience and purpose in mind.
7. Look at your page of support and identify your major subtopics.

   SUBTOPICS: _____

8. Choose an order for your subtopics, group your supporting information by subtopic, and eliminate any unnecessary information.

   ORDER: _____

9. Outline the body of your essay on a separate piece of paper.
10. Jot down ideas for the title, introduction, and conclusion.

Writing

Use your outline to write a complete first draft on a separate piece of paper. Keep your audience in mind as you write, and maintain an informative tone. Remember this is just a first draft.

Revising

Write *yes* or *no* to each of the following questions. Then rework your first draft to fix all the items marked *no*.

1. Does the title attract the reader's attention, suit the essay, and suggest the main point? _____
2. Does the introduction capture the reader's interest, provide necessary background information, establish a tone, and lead to the thesis statement? _____
3. Does the thesis statement present a clearly focused main point? _____
4. Does each body paragraph develop a significant subtopic and contain a topic sentence? _____
5. Does each body paragraph contain enough support? _____
6. Are the subtopics arranged in a logical order? _____
7. Are the ideas under each subtopic arranged in a logical order? _____
8. Does the conclusion recall the thesis statement and bring the essay to a satisfactory end? _____
9. Is the tone consistent and appropriate? _____
10. Are all the sentences grammatically correct? Are the sentences varied in length and structure? _____

After you have revised your essay, **proofread** it carefully and prepare an error-free final copy.

NAME _____ CLASS _____ DATE _____

19.3 Writing a Persuasive Essay

Prewriting

1. Write a suitable topic on the line below.

   TOPIC: _____

2. Identify your audience, making one up if necessary.

   AUDIENCE: _____

3. Focus your topic into a specific, supportable opinion.

   OPINION: _____

4. Now write your thesis statement.

   THESIS STATEMENT: _____

5. List the arguments supporting your opinion.

   SUPPORTING ARGUMENTS: _____
   _____
   _____

6. Now list the arguments against your opinion.

   OPPOSING ARGUMENTS: _____
   _____

7. Next list a counter-argument for each opposing argument.

   COUNTER-ARGUMENTS: _____
   _____

8. Now organize your arguments by order of importance.
9. Outline the body of your essay on a separate sheet of paper.
10. Jot down ideas for the title, introduction, and conclusion.

Writing

Use your outline to complete a first draft on a separate piece of paper. Begin by trying to capture the reader's interest and then move gradually toward your thesis statement. Try to maintain a reasonable, consistent tone, and avoid the use of emotional language. Remember this is just a first draft.

Prewriting

Write *yes* or *no* to each of the following questions. Then rework your first draft to fix all the items marked *no*.

1. Does the title attract the reader's attention, suit the essay, and suggest the main point? _____
2. Does your introduction capture the reader's interest and move gradually toward the thesis statement? _____
3. Are your arguments and ideas sound? _____
4. Is there enough information to support each argument? _____
5. Does the essay include opposing arguments? _____
6. Are the arguments well organized? _____
7. Does the conclusion recall the thesis statement and bring the essay to a satisfactory end? _____
8. Is the tone consistent and appropriate? _____
9. Is the essay interesting and convincing? _____
10. Are all the sentences grammatically correct? _____

After you have revised your essay, **proofread** it carefully and prepare an error-free final copy.

NAME _____ CLASS _____ DATE _____

19.3 Writing an Informal Essay

1. Choose a suitable topic and write it below.

   TOPIC: _____

2. Identify your audience, making one up if necessary.

   AUDIENCE: _____

3. State your main purpose.

   PURPOSE: _____

4. Decide on the type of tone you will use.

   TONE: _____

5. Next decide on your controlling idea.

   CONTROLLING IDEA: _____

6. On a separate piece of paper, make a list of information you can use to develop your controlling idea. Include any impressions, experiences, or personal responses that you want to use in your essay.
7. Now decide on a method of organization for your essay.

   ORGANIZATION: _____

8. Decide what types of linking devices you will use to tie your ideas together.

   LINKING DEVICES: _____

9. Outline your essay on a separate sheet of paper.
10. Decide on an appropriate title.

    TITLE: _____

Writing

Use your outline to write a first draft. Concentrate on maintaining a consistent tone and on linking your ideas subtly and smoothly. Remember this is only a first draft.

Revising

Write *yes* or *no* to each of the following questions. Then rework your first draft to improve all the items marked *no*.

1. Is the title appealing and appropriate? _____
2. Is your controlling idea made clear to the reader? _____
3. Have you included enough information to adequately develop your controlling idea? _____
4. Is the essay logically organized? _____
5. Is the tone consistent? _____
6. Are your ideas linked together subtly and smoothly? _____
7. Have you used the best words you can find to express your ideas? _____
8. Are all your sentences grammatically correct? _____

After revising your essay, **proofread** it carefully and prepare an error-free final copy.

NAME _____ CLASS _____ DATE _____

20.1 Understanding Research Papers

Sources of Information

Research papers include documented information from outside sources with footnotes at the bottom of the pages or at the end of the paper. Research papers must also contain a bibliography that reflects all the sources consulted during the research and planning stages of the paper.

Sample Footnote	Sample Bibliographic Entry
[2]Frank J. Sorauf, *Party Politics in America* (Boston: Little-Brown, 1976), p. 221.	Sorauf, Frank J., *Party Politics in America.* Boston: Little-Brown, 1976.

Structure and Features

A research paper has a title, an introduction with a thesis statement, a body, a conclusion, citations of sources throughout the paper, and a bibliography at the end.

Unity and Coherence

To achieve unity in research papers, reflect and develop your thesis statement in every paragraph. To achieve coherence, use your thesis statement to suggest a logical order for the body paragraphs; to maintain coherence, use transitions to combine research with your own ideas.

EXERCISE A: Using Sources of Information. Circle one of the topics below and use the library, the card catalog, and *The Readers' Guide* to write informal citations or footnotes for the kinds of sources described below.

Supreme Court   Communications satellites
European Economic Community   Life of Queen Victoria

1. An informal citation for a book

2. A footnote for a book

3. An informal citation for a magazine article

4. A footnote for an unsigned magazine article

5. A footnote for an encyclopedia article

EXERCISE B: Understanding the Structure and Features of a Research Paper. Answer each of these questions about a research paper.

1. What is the purpose of the introduction?

2. Where in the introduction should the thesis statement appear?

3. What should be used to determine a logical order for the body paragraphs?

4. How can the writer of a research paper avoid a charge of plagiarism?

5. Why is it important to include a comprehensive bibliography?

Copyright © by Prentice-Hall, Inc.

NAME _____ CLASS _____ DATE _____

20.2 Writing a Research Paper

Prewriting

1. Choose an interesting, narrow topic that can be supported with sufficient information.

   TOPIC: _____

2. Identify your audience, making one up if necessary.

   AUDIENCE: _____

3. Now state your purpose.

   PURPOSE: _____

4. On a separate piece of paper, write five key questions you plan to answer through research.
5. On the same sheet of paper, write a rough draft of your thesis statement.
6. On note cards, list complete information about each source you plan to use.
7. On note cards, take accurate notes to answer each of your questions.
8. Once you have researched your topic, revise your thesis statement to reflect your research.

   THESIS STATEMENT: _____

9. Decide which subtopics you want to cover.

   SUBTOPICS: _____

10. Organize your notes acording to subtopics.
11. Choose an order for your subtopics.

    ORDER: _____

12. On separate paper, prepare a formal outline for your paper.
13. Review your outline to see if there are places where your research could be stronger.

Writing

Using your outline and notes, write a complete first draft. Try to shape your paper without worrying about every detail since you will be revising. Do, however, include your informal citations or footnotes and prepare your bibliography.

Revising

Write *yes* or *no* to each question. Then revise your first draft to improve all the items marked *no*.

1. Have you included enough background material? _____
2. Does the thesis statement clearly indicate the paper's main point? _____
3. Does the information in the body thoroughly support and develop the main point? _____
4. Is the main idea of each body paragraph clear? _____
5. Do the body paragraphs develop your main point and subtopics in a logical order? Is all the information logically arranged within each paragraph? _____
6. Does the conclusion contain a restatement of summary of the paper's main point? Does it satisfactorily complete the paper? _____
7. Have you used complete citations for borrowed facts, ideas, and quotations? _____
8. Is your bibliography complete and correct? _____
9. Have you chosen your words carefully? Are your sentences varied? _____
10. Is your paper free of errors in grammar, usage, punctuation, and spelling? _____

After revising your paper, **proofread** it carefully and prepare an error-free final copy.

Copyright © by Prentice-Hall, Inc.

NAME _____ CLASS _____ DATE _____

21.1 Book Reports

Understanding Book Reports

A book report gives an informed overview of a work of fiction or nonfiction and offers an opinion of the book.

THE PARTS OF A BOOK REPORT	
Introduction	Gives the book's title and author and a brief summary of its contents
Body	Explores one or two of the book's literary elements
Conclusion	Offers an opinion of the book and advises the reader to read it or avoid it

EXERCISE A: Understanding a Book Report. Carefully read the book report below. Then answer the questions that follow it.

(1) *For Whom the Bell Tolls,* by Ernest Hemingway, is a captivating novel about love and war that has become a modern classic. Set in the mountains in Spain during the Spanish Civil War, the book focuses on an American man's attempts to play a role in overthrowing the fascist forces that had seized control of a sizable portion of the country.

(2) Robert Jordan, the protagonist, is a very brave and dedicated man. Because of his love for the Spanish people and his hatred for fascism, he left his safe, comfortable existence as a college professor to join the forces fighting the fascists in Spain. Without ever thinking of his own safety, he becomes entrenched in the conflict, using his knowledge of explosives to help the revolutionary cause. In the end, his loyalty and determination cost him his life.

(3) In this novel, Hemingway proposes that there is a relationship between love and death. Robert Jordan dies, as many of his comrades do, because of his love for Spain and its people. In the days before his death, he falls in love for the first time in his life with a young Spanish woman named Maria. Yet, throughout their brief love affair, there is a foreshadowing of doom. Realizing that he will probably die, Jordan relishes every moment he and Maria have together, hoping that the intensity of their love can make up for its lack of longevity. At the end of the novel, after he has been wounded and is certain to die, he demonstrates the depth of his love for Maria by refusing to let her endanger herself by staying with him. Jordan orders Maria to flee to safety, assuring her that he will live on forever inside of her heart.

(4) *For Whom the Bell Tolls* is a gripping suspenseful novel that anyone with an appreciation for quality fiction will enjoy. It is a masterpiece that will live on through the years as a classic American work of fiction.

1. What is the setting of the novel? _____
2. Who is the main character in the novel? _____
3. What happens to the main character at the end of the novel? _____
4. What is the theme of the novel? _____
5. What is the writer's overall evaluation of the novel? _____

EXERCISE B: More Work with Book Reports. Answer the following questions about the book report above.

1. What information is presented in the introduction? _____
2. What element of the novel is discussed in the second paragraph? _____
3. What element of the novel is discussed in the third paragraph? _____
4. Name one important element that is not discussed in the report. _____
5. What recommendation does the writer make? _____

NAME _____ CLASS _____ DATE _____

21.1 Writing a Book Report

Prewriting

1. Select a book that you have read recently.

   TITLE: _____ **AUTHOR:** _____

2. Choose two elements of the book to discuss.

   ELEMENTS: _____ _____

3. Gather and list supporting information for both elements.

   SUPPORTING INFORMATION: _____ _____
   _____ _____
   _____ _____
   _____ _____
   _____ _____
   _____ _____
   _____ _____

4. Decide what information you are going to present in your introduction.

   INTRODUCTION INFORMATION: _____
   _____

5. Decide what kind of evaluation you want to give in the conclusion.

   EVALUATION: _____

6. Choose an order for the elements you are going to discuss.

   ORDER: _____

7. On a separate piece of paper, use your list of supporting information and other notes to outline your report.

Writing

Use your outline to write a complete first draft on a separate sheet of paper. As you are writing, refer to your list of supporting ideas and concentrate on connecting your ideas with transitions.

Revising

Write *yes* or *no* to answer each of the following questions. Then rework your first draft to fix all the items marked *no*.

1. Are the author and title identified in the introduction? _____
2. Does the introduction give an overview of the book? _____
3. Do the elements discussed represent the book accurately? _____
4. Have you given enough supporting information to make your ideas clear to the reader? _____
5. Have you chosen the best support available in the book? _____
6. Is all the information relevant? _____
7. Have you used quotation marks correctly and given page numbers following any direct quotation from the book? _____
8. Does your conclusion contain a definite recommendation? _____
9. Does the paper read smoothly? _____
10. Is your paper free of errors in grammar, usage, punctuation and spelling? _____

After revising your paper, **proofread** it carefully and prepare an error-free final copy.

WRITING PROCESS PAGE

NAME _____ CLASS _____ DATE _____

21.2 Literary Analyses

Understanding Literary Analyses

A literary analysis broadens the reader's understanding of a work by explaining or interpreting it.

PARTS OF A LITERARY ANALYSIS PAPER	
Title	Suggests an aspect of the main point to be discussed
Introduction	Identifies the work and author, specifies the kind of work, clearly states the main point that will be made in the paper
Body	Explores subtopics of the main point and supports the main point with quotations, examples, and details
Conclusion	Recalls the main point in the introduction and pulls the paper together as a whole

EXERCISE A: Understanding a Literary Analysis Paper. Carefully read the paper below. Then answer the questions that follow.

The Downfall of Macbeth

(1) In Shakespeare's play *Macbeth,* the hero, Macbeth, brings about his own demise and destruction when he is driven by a promise of power to commit an act that violates his true nature. Macbeth murders the king of Scotland, and though he receives the crown after committing the act, his mind deteriorates into a chaotic state and he commits more evil acts in an attempt to suppress his guilty conscience and his growing paranoia.

(2) When Macbeth murders the king, Duncan, in an attempt to fulfill three witches' prediction that Macbeth will be the future king of Scotland, he violates his loyal, dedicated, and honest nature. Macbeth displays his true nature early in the play, declaring his dedication to the king: "The service, and the loyalty I owe."(I,iv,22) Macbeth is very hesitant when the time comes for him to follow through with his plan to kill Duncan, and he does so only after his wife has called him a coward and questioned his manhood. Once he has killed Duncan, Macbeth is filled with regret and he cries out, "Wake Duncan . . . I would thou couldst."(II,ii,74)

(3) After he has committed murder, Macbeth finds that he is overcome by a sense of guilt and paranoia that leads him to commit more evil acts that insure his eventual downfall and cause the country of Scotland to lapse into a state of chaos that parallels the state of Macbeth's mind. Living in a constant state of fear, Macbeth declares, "Ere we will eat our meal in fear, and sleep / In the affliction of these terrible dreams / That shake us nightly."(III,ii,17–19) In an attempt to appease his anxiety, Macbeth commits more murders, but he only finds that his control is continuing to slip away. At the same time, Macbeth's actions cause the entire country to deteriorate into a state of chaos, and Ross, a Scottish nobleman, declares that Scotland "cannot / be called our mother, but our grave."(IV,iii,165–166)

(4) When Macbeth responded to a promise of power by killing Duncan he ensured his own eventual demise and destruction. Committing the act violated Macbeth's nature and elicited a deep sense of guilt within him that led him to murder again and caused Scotland to lapse into a chaotic state.

1. What is the main point stated in the introduction? _____
2. How does the title help prepare the reader for the main point? _____
3. What other information is presented in the introduction? _____
4. What subtopic is discussed in the second paragraph? _____
5. What subtopic is discussed in the third paragraph? _____

EXERCISE B: More Work with Literary Analysis. Answer the following questions about the paper.

1. How is the first subtopic related to the main idea? _____
2. How is the second subtopic related to the main idea? _____
3. Give an example of supporting information presented under the first subtopic. _____
4. Give an example of supporting information presented under the second subtopic. _____
5. Which sentence in the conclusion refers back to the main point? _____

NAME _____ CLASS _____ DATE _____

21.2 Writing a Literary Analysis

Prewriting

1. Choose a work that lends itself to in-depth literary analysis.

   TITLE: _____ **AUTHOR:** _____

2. Examine various elements and decide which element or elements you want to focus on.

   ELEMENT(S): _____

3. Decide on your audience (people who have or have not read the work, and so on).

   AUDIENCE: _____

4. Decide on your purpose (to inform, persuade, and so on).

   PURPOSE: _____

5. Write a thesis statement.

   THESIS STATEMENT: _____

6. Gather information from the work to support your thesis statement.
7. Decide on your subtopics (the elements or aspects of an element).

   SUBTOPICS: _____

8. Choose an order for your subtopics (order of importance, developmental, and so on).

   ORDER: _____

9. Outline the body of your paper.
10. Jot down ideas for your title, introduction, and conclusion.

Writing

Using your outline, write a complete first draft of your analysis. Try to shape your paper without worrying about every detail since you will revise it. Try, however, to discuss what you planned without going off on a tangent.

Revising

Write *yes* or *no* to each of the following questions. Then revise your first draft to improve all the items marked *no*.

1. Have you chosen the best title for your paper? _____
2. Do the introductory statements provide enough background and summary information? _____
3. Does your thesis statement present your main point and indicate the paper's purpose? _____
4. Do the subtopics develop the main point with sufficient examples, details, and quotations? _____
5. Have you identified all direct quotations and used one consistent method for citing sources? _____
6. Does the conclusion include a reminder of the main point and bring the paper to a satisfactory close? _____
7. Have you used transitions and other devices needed for coherence? _____
8. Throughout the paper, is your analysis centered on the work and presented clearly? _____
9. Are sentences varied in length and structure? _____
10. Is your paper free of errors in grammar, usage, mechanics, and spelling? _____

After revising your paper, **proofread** it carefully and prepare an error-free final copy.

NAME _____ CLASS _____ DATE _____

22.1 Journals

Understanding Journals

A journal is a personal record of events, feelings, insights, and observations; often, it reflects the writer's special interests.

KINDS OF JOURNALS	
Purposes of Journals	**Probable Writing time**
To keep track of everyday events	Daily
To express candid feelings and insights	Daily or several times weekly
To record key events or moments in life	Weekly
To record experiences in an area of special interest	As each occasion arises

Keeping a Journal

Use vivid sensory details as you record events chronologically in your journal.

EXERCISE A: Understanding the Purpose of Journal Entries. Read each item below and determine the purpose of the journal the writer is keeping.

EXAMPLE: This morning I overslept and was late for school.
To keep track of everyday events

1. Playing the role of Ophelia in *Hamlet* was very challenging. _____
2. I can't escape feeling depressed since my father left home. _____
3. Today's game was even more exciting than yesterday's. _____
4. Traveling to New York City for the day on Tuesday was the highlight of my week. _____
5. I really think that I'm falling in love with Roger, but I'm afraid to tell him how I feel about him. _____

EXERCISE B: Planning a Journal Entry. Choose one of the topics below or a topic of your own. Then answer the questions that follow to plan a journal entry.

    Losing a close friend   Hiding your emotions
    Feeling anxious about an upcoming event   Going to a place you've never been to

1. When? _____
2. Who? _____
3. Where? _____
4. What? _____

5. Your reactions? _____

NAME _____ CLASS _____ DATE _____

22.2 Writing an Anecdote

Prewriting

1. Select an event from your own experience to write about.

   EVENT: _____

2. Identify the setting.

   SETTING: _____

3. Now identify your reason for sharing this experience.

   REASON: _____

4. List the incidents that you use in your anecdote in chronological order.

   INCIDENTS: _____
   _____
   _____
   _____

5. Now list the major characters that you want to include.

   CHARACTERS: _____
   _____

6. Think of some descriptive details that will enliven your anecdote for your readers.

   DESCRIPTIVE DETAILS: _____
   _____
   _____

Writing

Use your list of incidents, characters, and descriptive details to write a first draft of your anecdote. As you write, continue brainstorming for pertinent details that you may have missed in your outline. Remember that this is only a first draft and that you will have an opportunity to improve it.

Revising

Write *yes* or *no* to answer each of the following questions. Then revise your first draft to improve all the items marked *no*.

1. Is it clear whether your anecdote is complete in itself or part of a larger composition? _____
2. Does it focus on one major event? _____
3. Do the incidents follow chronological order with a clear beginning, middle, and conclusion? _____
4. Will readers understand why you have shared this event with them? Does the conclusion make that clear? _____
5. Do descriptive details and dialogue enliven the anecdote? _____
6. Is the first-person point of view maintained throughout? _____
7. Is your paper free of errors in grammar, spelling, usage, and mechanics? _____

After revising your paper, **proofread** it carefully and prepare an error-free final copy.

NAME _____ CLASS _____ DATE _____

22.2 Writing a First-Person Narrative

Prewriting

1. Choose a topic for your narrative.

TOPIC: _____

2. Identify the setting.

SETTING: _____

3. List the incidents that you will include in your narrative.

INCIDENTS: _____
_____
_____
_____
_____

4. Arrange the incidents in chronological order.
5. List the characters that you want to include.

CHARACTERS: _____
_____

6. Now list the personal observations that you want to include.

OBSERVATIONS: _____
_____
_____

7. Next, think of some descriptive details that will enliven your narrative for your readers.

DESCRIPTIVE DETAILS: _____
_____
_____

Writing

Use your lists of incidents, observations, and descriptive details to write a first draft of your narrative. As you write, keep in mind the key features of a first-person narrative and concentrate on maintaining a clear chronological presentation. Remember that this is only a first draft and that you will have an opportunity to improve it.

Revising

Write *yes* or *no* to each of the following questions. Then rework your first draft to fix all the items marked *no*.

1. Does your narrative stick to its subject without straying? _____
2. Do the events follow chronological order with transitions to connect ideas? _____
3. Does the narrative have a clear beginning, a logical development, and a satisfying conclusion? _____
4. Do descriptive details and dialogue enliven the work? _____
5. Have you included personal observations or feelings about your subject? _____
6. Did you maintain a consistent first-person point of view throughout? _____
7. Is your paper free of errors in grammar, usage, mechanics, and spelling? _____

After revising your paper, **proofread** it carefully and prepare an error-free final copy.

22.2 Writing an Autobiography

Prewriting

1. Decide on the time span your autobiography will cover.

   TIME SPAN: _____

2. Now identify the setting.

   SETTING: _____

3. Next, list the events you will focus on.

   EVENTS: _____
   _____

4. Now arrange the events in chronological order.
5. List the characters you want to include.

   CHARACTERS: _____
   _____

6. Select some descriptive details about the setting you have chosen to help you visualize what you are writing about.

   DETAILS: _____
   _____

7. Select some descriptive details about the characters you have chosen.

   DETAILS: _____
   _____

8. Write some of your personal reactions to the events you have chosen.

   PERSONAL REACTIONS: _____
   _____

Writing

Use the plan you have sketched above to write a first draft of your autobiography. Concentrate on presenting events and details from a consistent first-person point of view to give the reader a clear idea of what was happening and how you felt about it. Remember that this is only a first draft and that you will have an opportunity to improve it.

Revising

Write *yes* or *no* to answer each of the following questions. Then rework your first draft to fix all the items marked *no*.

1. Is the time span of your autobiography clear? _____
2. Do the events follow chronological order? _____
3. Do you maintain a consistent first-person point of view? _____
4. Have you included vivid descriptions? _____
5. Have you included personal feelings and observations? _____
6. Does your autobiography reach a satisfying conclusion? _____
7. Is your autobiography free of errors in grammar, usage, mechanics, and spelling? _____

After revising your paper, **proofread** it carefully and prepare an error-free final copy.

NAME _____ CLASS _____ DATE _____

23.1 Understanding Short Stories

Character and Plot

In a short story, a writer tries to establish one clear, dominant impression about each important character. The plot of a story is a chain of events which flow from a central conflict.

STAGES OF A PLOT	
Exposition	Introduces the characters and places them in a setting; establishes a point of view; fills in background information
Opening Incident	Creates a central conflict and starts the plot moving
Rising Action	Adds new incidents or insights to intensify conflict
Climax	Raises the conflict to maximum intensity; changes the course of events or the reader's understanding
Falling Action	Relaxes conflict to prepare readers for the conclusion
Conclusion	Resolves the conflict; carries the plot to an end, often interpreting the story or giving a final insight

Point of View

The point of view must be unified and consistent in a well-structured short story.

KINDS OF NARRATORS	
First person	The narrator tells the story as he or she saw it and usually participates in the action.
Limited Third Person	The narrator is outside the story and cannot see into the characters' minds.
Omniscient Third Person	The narrator is outside the story but is able to see into the characters' minds.

EXERCISE A: Recognizing the Stages of a Plot. Identify each item below as (1) exposition, (2) opening incident, (3) rising action, (4) climax, or (5) conclusion.

EXAMPLE: The shadow moved closer and I could feel my heart-rate accelerating. __3__

1. Joe awoke filled with excitement as the sun was rising. ____
2. Thrashing about and gasping for air, Joe was losing strength, and, in a state of terror, he was becoming certain that he was going to drown. ____
3. Just as Joe was about to give up his fight for survival, a lifeguard reached him and began towing him back to shore. ____
4. While Joe lay on the sand, still gasping for air, he decided he would never try surfing again. ____
5. Joe approached the rental shop and asked for a surfboard. ____

EXERCISE B: Identifying Kinds of Narrators. Identify the point of view expressed in each item below as (1) first person, (2) limited third person, or (3) omniscient third person.

EXAMPLE: I struggled to think of a plausible excuse. __1__

1. Sue wondered whether she would finish on time. ____
2. Jim and Bill stepped aside as the dignitaries passed. ____
3. Lois thought that if she stayed perfectly still no one would notice her. ____
4. I could not believe that I had overlooked such an obvious clue. ____
5. Phil winced slightly as the doctor pressed the needle into his arm. ____

NAME _____ CLASS _____ DATE _____

23.1 Understanding Short Stories

Dialogue
Dialogue helps a short story writer to make characters believable and to advance the plot.

Language and Tone
A writer must choose language and create a tone that is both appropriate and consistent.

Problems in Tone	Improvements
Euphemism: The widow brought flowers to the memorial park.	The widow brought flowers to the cemetery.
Overly Formal Language: The instructional staff conducted a meeting before school.	The teachers met before school.
Slang: Rose doesn't really get off on jazz.	Rose doesn't really like jazz.
Specialized Language: Jake's fractured radius will keep him out for the rest of the season.	Jake's broken wrist will keep him out for the rest of the season.
Foreign Phrase: Several of Rembrandt's chefs-d'oeuvre are in the exhibit.	Several of Rembrandt's masterpieces are in the exhibit.
Inappropriate Connotation: The driver deviated to avoid the dog.	The driver swerved to avoid the dog.

EXERCISE A: Working with Dialogue. Rewrite each item below in dialogue form.

EXAMPLE: Isabella promised that the orders would be delivered by Christmas.
"I promise that all orders will be delivered by Christmas," vowed Isabella.

1. Mrs. Hackensack scolded her daughter for making such a mess.
   _____
2. Jerome apologized for being late to class.
   _____
3. Dudley asked Barbara out to dinner.
   _____
4. Sandy recommended that the group vote on the two plans.
   _____
5. Leroy warned Ron not to bother him while he was working.
   _____

EXERCISE B: Understanding Language and Tone. Underline the word(s) in each item that creates a problem in tone. Then write an appropriate replacement for the underlined word(s).

EXAMPLE: Jenkins shows a *proclivity* toward music.   *inclination*

1. Dr. Mead's acceptance of the leadership position is the sine qua non of a successful expedition. _____
2. Ben was really uptight about taking the entrance exam. _____
3. The salad dressing is basically an amalgam of oil and vinegar. _____
4. The coach's speech at half time really fired up his team. _____
5. A custodial officer closed the cell door behind the prisoner. _____

Copyright © by Prentice-Hall, Inc.

NAME _____ CLASS _____ DATE _____

23.2 Writing a Story

Prewriting

1. Decide on the main character of your story.

   MAIN CHARACTER: _____

2. Write down key details about your main character.

   CHARACTER DETAILS: _____
   _____

3. Now list the other major characters that you will include in your story.

   MAJOR CHARACTERS: _____
   _____

4. Decide what kind of conflict your main character will become involved in. Then state your conflict in a single sentence.

   CONFLICT: _____

5. Write down some details of the setting, including time and place.

   SETTING: _____

6. Next, decide on the kind of narrator you will use.

   POINT OF VIEW: _____

7. Prepare a plot outline based on character and conflict.

   EXPOSITION: _____
   OPENING INCIDENT: _____
   RISING ACTION: _____
   CLIMAX: _____
   FALLING ACTION: _____
   CONCLUSION: _____

Writing

Use your plot outline to write a first draft of your story, maintaining a consistent point of view. Concentrate on connecting the events with transitions and on making the dialogue fit your characters and situations. Remember that this is only a first draft and that you will have an opportunity to improve it.

Revising

Write *yes* or *no* to answer each of the following questions. Then revise your first draft to improve all the items marked *no*.

1. Is the point of view clear and consistent? _____
2. Is the narrator's tone appropriate for the point of view? _____
3. Have you used sensory details to establish an appropriate mood? _____
4. Is the conflict clear? _____
5. Is the development of the plot logical throughout? _____
6. Does the conflict build through rising action? _____
7. Does the dialogue sound the way the characters would speak? _____
8. Is your paper free of errors in grammar, usage, mechanics, and spelling? _____

After revising your paper, **proofread** it carefully and prepare an error-free final copy.

NAME _____ CLASS _____ DATE _____

24.1 Personal Letters

Understanding Personal Letters

Personal letters contain a heading, a salutation, a body, a closing, and a signature. Use either indented or semiblock style for your personal letters.

PERSONAL LETTER STYLES	
Indented	Heading, closing, and signature are *not* lined up vertically.
Semiblock	Heading, closing, and signature are lined up vertically.

Writing Personal Letters

Organize the information you want to share in a friendly letter. Focus on your purpose when writing a social note.

SUGGESTIONS FOR WRITING FRIENDLY LETTERS
1. Answer any questions the recipient asked in his or her last letter.
2. Mention previous letters, visits, or phone calls.
3. Use facts and details about people, places, and events.
4. Proofread your letter carefully.

EXERCISE A: Working with the Parts of a Social Letter. Follow the instructions below.

1. Write two headings, the first in indented style and the second in semiblock.

2. Write two salutations, one to a relative and the other to a friend.

3. Write two closings and signatures, one in indented style, the other in semiblock.

4. Which parts of a friendly letter begin on the right? _____

5. Which parts begin on the left? _____

EXERCISE B: Planning a Friendly Letter. Complete the following prewriting activities.

1. Write the name of someone you could write a personal letter to. _____
2. List some interests or shared experiences that you and this person have in common. _____
3. List one piece of information or one idea that you could tell this person about. _____
4. List one recent event that you could tell this person about. _____
5. List any questions you could ask this person. _____

Copyright © by Prentice-Hall, Inc.

NAME _____ CLASS _____ DATE _____

24.2 Business Letters

Understanding Business Letters

A business letter should include six basic parts: a heading, an inside address, a salutation, a body, a closing, and a signature. Use block style, modified block style, or semiblock style for your business letters.

SPECIAL RULES FOR BUSINESS LETTERS

1. Use 8½" × 11" white bond paper and standard matching envelopes.
2. Type your business letter, if possible.
3. Follow one format consistently in your letter and on your envelope.
4. Leave a one-inch margin on all sides of your paper.

Writing Business Letters

Write business letters that explain your purpose quickly and directly.

TYPES OF BUSINESS LETTERS

Types	Contents
Request	Polite request for specific information or other material
Order	Very specific request, detailing number, price, method of payment, and so on
Complaint	Request to adjust an order or correct a mistake
Opinion	Letter stating views clearly with solid supporting reasons

EXERCISE A: Working with the Parts of a Business Letter. Follow the instructions below.

1. Write two inside addresses.

   _____   _____
   _____   _____
   _____   _____

2. Write two salutations.

   _____   _____

3. In which style does everything begin on the left? _____
4. What should go at the top of the second page? _____
5. What should appear two or three spaces below the body of a business letter? _____
   _____

EXERCISE B: Planning a Business Letter. Choose one of the types of business letters in the chart above. Then complete the prewriting activities below.

1. What is the purpose of your business letter? _____
2. Who is the audience of your letter? _____
3. What essential information should be included? _____
4. List specific information (that you make up) in the order in which you would write it in the letter.

   _____
   _____
   _____

5. Write the first sentence of your letter. _____

NAME _____ CLASS _____ DATE _____

24.3 Applications

Interpreting the Question
Determine the specific requirements of an essay question on an application.

QUESTIONS ON COLLEGE APPLICATIONS	
Topical Questions	Ask for your understanding, interpretation, or stand on some idea of general interest
Goal Questions	Ask for specific ideas about your future, as a college student and after graduation
Personal Questions	Ask for background information about your school and personal life

Preparing Your Answers
Follow the steps for planning, writing, and revising a paragraph or essay when writing on an application.

STEPS IN PLANNING AN ANSWER
1. Analyze the question.
2. Decide on the length of your answer.
3. Write a sentence that gives the main point of your response and suggests your purpose.
4. Think of supporting information that is appropriate for your purpose.

EXERCISE A: Recognizing the Types of Questions on College Applications. Identify each question below as (1) topical, (2) goal, or (3) personal.

EXAMPLE: What is your favorite activity outside of school? Why? __3__

1. Why do you feel that a college education is important? _____
2. What is the best book you have ever read? Why? _____
3. What extracurricular activities do you expect to become involved in while you are in college? Why? _____
4. What was your favorite subject in high school? Why? _____
5. At this point, what do you plan to do once you graduate from college? _____

EXERCISE B: Planning an Answer to a Question on a College Application. Choose one of the questions from Exercise A. Then complete the prewriting activities below.

1. Decide on the main point you want to make in your answer. _____

_____

2. Decide on the length of your answer. _____

3. Write your topic sentence or thesis statement. _____

_____

4. Write three examples of facts, details, or reasons that you can use to support your main point.

_____

_____

_____

Copyright © by Prentice-Hall, Inc.

NAME _____ CLASS _____ DATE _____

25.1 Essay Exams

Getting Started

Allot time for the parts of an exam, recognizing that essay questions take several planning and writing steps. Use word clues to determine the kind of question being asked.

Kind of Question	Word Clue	Kind of Question	Word Clue
Compare	compare, similarities resemblances, likenesses	Explanation Illustration	explain, why, what, how illustrate, show
Contrast	contrast, differ, differences	Interpretation	significance, meaning of, quotations or events, influence, analyze
Definition	define, explain		
Description	describe	Opinion	what do you think, defend your idea, state your opinion
Diagram	diagram, draw, chart		
Discussion	discuss, explain		
		Prediction	If . . . then; What . . . if

EXERCISE A: Budgeting Your Time. Assume you have forty-five minutes to answer two essay questions. List below the steps you will follow and the amount of time for each.

Steps   Time Allocation

EXERCISE B: Interpreting a Question. Read the following essay question and answer the questions that follow.

Twentieth-century fiction is concerned with areas of experience, states of consciousness, and a variety of themes that the novel did not deal with before. Select *two* American novelists and *one* British novelist and describe the extent to which their work reflects the statement above. In your answer refer to at least *two* novels by *each* author.

1. How many novelists must you include? _____
2. How many novels should you mention? _____
3. What twentieth-century elements should you look for in each?
   _____

4. What should you focus on in your topic sentence or thesis statement?
   _____

5. How should you support your answer?
   _____

142   Copyright © by Prentice-Hall, Inc.

NAME _____ CLASS _____ DATE _____

25.1 Essay Exams

Planning, Writing, and Checking Your Answer

State your main idea in one sentence, and then list supporting ideas and information.

STEPS IN PLANNING AN ANSWER
1. Decide on a main idea or main point.
2. List as much support as possible.
3. Organize your support in a modified outline.

EXERCISE A: Planning an Answer. Choose one of the following questions, circle it, and plan a paragraph-length answer by completing the steps below.

What are the two most important functions served by television?

Why do you think so many Americans fail to vote?

1. What main idea will you present at the beginning of your answer? _____

2. What support will you offer? _____

3. What order will you use for your support? _____

EXERCISE B: Writing and Checking an Answer. In the space below, write the answer you planned in Exercise A. Then check it carefully and make any necessary corrections.

_____

Copyright © by Prentice-Hall, Inc.

NAME _____ CLASS _____ DATE _____

25.2 Précis

Understanding Précis

A précis preserves the main ideas, details, purpose, organization, and tone of an original work, using different words.

CHARACTERISTICS OF A PRÉCIS	
Original work is reduced in size	Follows same pattern of organization
Retains main ideas, purpose, and tone of original	Is reworded carefully by the précis writer

Preparing a Précis

Read the original several times and take notes. Write a first draft that reflects the author's ideas, purpose, and tone. Revise carefully, checking for accuracy.

EXERCISE A: Understanding a Précis. Answer each question.

1. What is the major purpose of a précis?

2. Before beginning a précis, what should you do?

3. What features of the original work should you strive to retain?

4. In choosing the language for the précis, what must you do?

5. What should you do when you revise your first draft?

EXERCISE B: Planning a Précis. Find and read a long editorial, a lengthy book review, or an article in a scientific or historical journal. Plan to write a précis by completing the items below.

1. What is the name of the original work?

2. What main ideas does it include?

3. What do you think is its purpose?

4. How would you describe its tone?

5. What is its pattern of organization?

NAME _____ CLASS _____ DATE _____

26.1 Techniques for Building Vocabulary

Making Good Use of Resource Material

Use a dictionary to find meaning, spelling, and proper pronunciation of words. Use a thesaurus to find words that are similar in meaning.

Dictionary	Thesaurus
Spelling: bois-ter-ous Pronunciation: (bois′ tər əs) Meaning: loud and exuberant	Words similar in meaning: boisterous: excited, noisy, rampageous

Recognizing Related Words

Synonyms are words similar in meaning; antonyms are words opposite in meaning; homonyms are words that sound alike but have different meanings.

Synonyms	Antonyms	Homonyms
resist/oppose	dishonest/virtuous	weigh/way

EXERCISE A: Using a Dictionary and a Thesaurus to Increase Vocabulary. Use a dictionary to look up the definition of each word below, and write the definition in the space provided. Then use a thesaurus to find a synonym for each word.

EXAMPLE: ardent   _intensely enthusiastic_   _zealous_

Word	Definition	Synonym
1. hypocrisy	_____	_____
2. tremulous	_____	_____
3. debilitate	_____	_____
4. vociferous	_____	_____
5. paradoxical	_____	_____
6. anomaly	_____	_____
7. ebullient	_____	_____
8. malevolent	_____	_____
9. scurrilous	_____	_____
10. diminution	_____	_____

EXERCISE B: Recognizing Related Words. Identify each set of words as synonyms, antonyms, or homonyms.

EXAMPLE: daring/defiant   _synonyms_

1. mite/might _____
2. obedience/compliance _____
3. discourteous/thoughtful _____
4. ecstasy/happiness _____
5. complicate/disentangle _____
6. notorious/inconspicuous _____
7. rhyme/rime _____
8. royalty/payment _____
9. earn/urn _____
10. outline/describe _____

Copyright © by Prentice-Hall, Inc.

NAME _____ CLASS _____ DATE _____

26.1 Techniques for Building Vocabulary

Remembering Vocabulary Words

Use one or more review techniques to remember the meanings of new words.

STUDYING AND REVIEWING METHODS
1. Set up an individual three-column vocabulary notebook.
2. Use index cards to make a set of flash cards.
3. Work with a tape recorder.
4. Study with a partner.
5. Group your list of words into sets of four or five.
6. Set daily or weekly goals for improving your vocabulary.

EXERCISE A: Using the Three-Column Method. Use your imagination to fill in the missing bridge words (words that act as hints of the definitions). Use a dictionary to fill in the missing definitions.

EXAMPLE: plankton ___food___ minute plants and animals on which ocean fish feed

1. demographer	_____	student of human population
2. estuary	flood	_____
3. inert	_____	inactive
4. disparity	_____	lack of equality
5. alleviate	all over	_____
6. emeritus	merit	_____
7. steppe	_____	vast, dry, level grassland
8. feasible	feat	_____
9. aficionado	_____	devoted follower
10. inherent	heritage	_____

EXERCISE B: Using Other Study Methods. Use a dictionary to look up the definition of each word below, and write the definition in the space provided. Copy each word on one side of an index card. On the other side, copy its definition. Work with a partner, quizzing each other on the definitions.

EXAMPLE: recoil ___to draw back___

Word   Definition
1. surmise _____
2. haughty _____
3. censorious _____
4. odious _____
5. propriety _____
6. litigious _____
7. clamorous _____
8. blasphemous _____
9. subservient _____
10. heterogeneous _____

26.2 Using Context

Recognizing Context Clues

Use context clues in all of your reading to improve both your vocabulary and your reading comprehension.

> **USING CONTEXT CLUES**
> 1. Read the sentence, omitting the unfamiliar word.
> 2. Look for clues within the sentence.
> 3. Guess the meaning of the unfamiliar word and substitute your guess in the sentence
> 4. Use a dictionary to check your guess.

Using Context Clues in Textbook Reading

Use context clues to determine the meanings of unfamiliar words in your textbook reading.

Using Context Clues in Other Kinds of Reading

Use context clues to determine the meanings of unfamiliar words in your reading of informative or analytic material.

EXERCISE A: Using Context Clues. Read the passage below. Then circle the correct meaning of each underlined word.

When you consider the (1) <u>primacy</u> of good vision in every day life, you will recognize the service (2) <u>optometrists</u> perform in (3) <u>rectifying</u> vision problems. To (4) <u>ameliorate</u> vision, an optometrist prescribes various aids. His goal is to <u>enhance</u> visual (5) <u>acuity</u>. Cases of (6) <u>ocular</u> (7) <u>pathology</u>, or eye diseases, are treated by an (8) <u>ophthalmologist</u>. When an optometrist discovers an ocular (9) <u>anomaly</u>, he refers a patient to a medical specialist. Sometimes optometrists work in (10) <u>conjunction</u> with other medical professionals to promote the overall health of a patient.

EXAMPLE: enhance (a) solve; (b) understand; ((c) improve,) (d) enable
1. primacy: (a) primary; (b) specialty; (c) importance; (d) passage
2. optometrist: (a) specialist in vision care; (b) eye surgeon; (c) lens maker; (d) pathologist
3. rectifying: (a) correcting; (b) retraining; (c) replacing; (d) hiding
4. ameliorate: (a) approve; (b) improve; (c) diagnose; (d) recognize
5. acuity: (a) guidance; (b) regularity; (c) keenness; (d) uniformity
6. ocular: (a) related to the nerves; (b) disease; (c) vision; (d) related to the eyes
7. pathology: (a) patients; (b) disease; (c) corrective; (d) treatment
8. ophthalmologist: (a) brain surgeon; (b) eye disease specialist; (c) health specialist; (d) social worker
9. anomaly: (a) affect; (b) annoyance; (c) fatigue; (d) irregularity
10. conjunction: (a) context; (b) theory; (c) combination; (d) care

EXERCISE B: More Work with Context Clues. Write a definition for each underlined word. Then check your definition in a dictionary.

EXAMPLE: Her <u>timorous</u> voice revealed her fearful nature. ___anxious___
1. He must be <u>daft</u> to attempt such a dangerous climb. _____
2. He is generous, but his uncle is <u>parsimonious</u>. _____
3. Her <u>terse</u> remarks were short and succinct. _____
4. Her nature was <u>placid</u>, like a calm and peaceful day. _____
5. Some parts of the book are clear, but others are <u>abstruse</u>. _____

26.3 Using Structure

Prefixes

Learn the meanings of common prefixes to improve your vocabulary and reading comprehension.

TWENTY COMMON PREFIXES			
ab- (a-, abs-)	away, from	over-	above, in excess
com- (co-, col-, con-, cor-)	with, together	post-	after
de-	away from, off	pre-	before
dis- (di-, dif-)	away, apart	re-	back, again
epi-	upon, over	semi-	half, partly
ex- (e-, ec-, ef-)	forth, from, out	sub- (suc-, suf-, sup-)	beneath, under
in- (il-, im-, ir-)	not	super-	above
inter-	between	syn- (syl-, sum-, sys-)	with
mis-	wrong	trans-	across
mono-	alone, one	un-	not

EXERCISE A: Using Prefixes to Define Words. Circle the definition that best fits each word. Check your answers in a dictionary.

EXAMPLE: abduct: (a) remove by force; (b) lead towards; (c) force to agree; (d) reduce

1. transpose: (a) model; (b) shift; (c) move back; (d) increase
2. postnatal: (a) undelivered; (b) before birth; (c) elaborate column; (d) after birth
3. abrogate: (a) absolute; (b) summary; (c) cancel; (d) border
4. intermediary: (a) go-between; (b) interval; (c) medical; (d) spacious
5. syndrome: (a) set of symptoms; (b) words; (c) synonyms; (d) meetings
6. demoralize: (a) demolish; (b) balance; (c) exercise; (d) discourage
7. monosyllable: (a) song; (b) single mark; (c) one syllable; (d) several syllables
8. immoderate: (a) excessive; (b) immune; (c) detailed; (d) modest
9. epilogue: (a) concluding section; (b) epistle; (c) bonus; (d) outer layer
10. preceding: (a) dignified; (b) leaving; (c) former; (d) separate

EXERCISE B: Using Prefixes to Make Words. Use each prefix below to create a word. Then write the definition of the word. Check your definition in a dictionary.

EXAMPLE: mis-
    misinterpret   _interpret wrongly_

1. mis- _____   _____
2. un- _____   _____
3. com- _____   _____
4. dis- _____   _____
5. over- _____   _____
6. re- _____   _____
7. sub- _____   _____
8. ex- _____   _____
9. semi- _____   _____
10. super- _____   _____

NAME _____ CLASS _____ DATE _____

26.3 Using Structure

Roots

Learn the meanings of common roots to improve your vocabulary and reading comprehension.

TEN COMMON ROOTS			
-dic- (-dict-)	to say	-scrib- (-script-)	to write
-graph-	to write	-spec- (-spect-)	to see
-mit- (-mis-)	to send	-ten- (-tain-, -tin-)	to hold
-plic- (-pli-)	to fold	-vad- (-vas-)	to go
-puls- (-pel-)	to drive	-vert- (-vers-)	to turn

Suffixes

Learn the meanings of common suffixes to improve your vocabulary and reading comprehension.

TEN COMMON SUFFIXES			
-ac (-ic)	characteristic of (noun or adjective)	-ism	characteristic of the theory of (noun)
-ate	making, applying (verb)	-ive	tending to (noun or adjective)
-ful	full of (noun or adjective)	-ize	to make (verb)
-fy	to make (verb)	-less	without (adjective)
-ish	belonging to, rather (adjective)	-ly	in a certain way (adjective or adverb)

EXERCISE A: Using Roots to Define Words. Circle the two words in each sentence that have the same root and underline the root. Then write a definition of each word and check your definition in a dictionary.

EXAMPLE: None of the (employees) were (implicated) in the scheme.
_____workers, shown to be involved_____

1. To what extent are you pretending? _____
2. This manual explains how we manufacture our product. _____
3. The spectators were treated to a breathtaking spectacle. _____
4. I saw the inventor at a recent convention. _____
5. Because of a defect, this product is ineffective. _____
6. Nothing can induce me to conduct this experiment. _____
7. We will not subject you to possible rejection. _____
8. I cannot conceive of an exception to that rule. _____
9. This inquest is required by law. _____
10. My portable typewriter is imported from France. _____

EXERCISE B: Using Suffixes to Form New Words. Add a suffix to each word listed below to give it the meaning listed at the right.

EXAMPLE: possess _____possessive_____ tending to possess

1. change _____ capable of being changed
2. real _____ result of showing reality
3. budget _____ pertaining to the budget
4. mourn _____ full of sorrow
5. civil _____ to make tame

26.4 Exploring Etymologies

Borrowed Words

Loanwords are words in the English language that have been borrowed from other languages.

BORROWED WORDS		
Latin—delirium	Greek—microscope	Italian—balcony
Spanish—vanilla	Russian—vodka	Persian—caravan

Words with New Meanings

The English language grows by giving new meaning to old words. Additionally, many new words are added to the language when two existing words are joined together to form a third word with a new meaning.

Coined Words

The English language grows through the addition of newly coined words. There are a variety of methods by which new words are coined.

TYPES OF COINED WORDS	
Words from Proper Nouns	New words based on the names of people, places, or characters in stories
Portmanteau Words	Words that "pack" the meanings of two other words into one word
Clipped Words	Shortened versions of longer words
Brand Names	Brand names of products and services that are used for all similar items

EXERCISE A: Finding the Sources of Words. Look up each of the following words in a dictionary. If the word is a borrowed word, write the language of origin. If it is a coined word, write the word or words of origin.

EXAMPLE: exterior ___Latin___

1. Jeffersonian _____
2. agent _____
3. curie _____
4. sherbet _____
5. smog _____
6. komondor _____
7. jello _____
8. ageism _____
9. offensive _____
10. jibe _____

EXERCISE B: Combining Words to Create New Words. Combine a word from the following list with each numbered word to create a new word.

    board   ear   wash   main   apple
    egg   snake   moon   mail   shift

EXAMPLE: sea ___seaboard___

1. plant _____
2. air _____
3. cup _____
4. light _____
5. hog _____
6. sauce _____
7. make _____
8. drum _____
9. land _____
10. skin _____

NAME _____ CLASS _____ DATE _____

27.1 Techniques for Improving Spelling

Proofreading Carefully
Proofread everything you write for spelling errors. Use a dictionary to look up words that you suspect may be wrong.

Studying Spelling Demons
Review a list of spelling demons to identify words you may have problems spelling correctly.

COMMON SPELLING DEMONS				
acquaintance	conscientious	immigrant	mischievous	possession
psychology	ridiculous	sergeant	symmetrical	unnecessary

EXERCISE A: Proofreading a Selection. There are ten misspelled words in the paragraph below. Find each misspelled word and spell it correctly in one of the spaces provided below the paragraph.

   Each year, thousands of young men and women graduate from college and move into a wide variety of profesions. Many choose to go into buisness, working for large corporations as bookeepers, accountants, and economic forecasters. They dream of someday becoming millionares and owning expensive cars and vacation houses. Others are less concerned with money, and try to find jobs that they feel will be benefical to individual people or will help society as a whole. Men and women with these concerns often become psycologists, teachers, and social workers. Other recent college graduates try to play a role in solving envirnmental problems, such as polution. There are also a few young men and women who are intrested in English and find jobs editing grammer and composition textbooks.

1. _____
2. _____
3. _____
4. _____
5. _____
6. _____
7. _____
8. _____
9. _____
10. _____

EXERCISE B: Mastering Spelling Demons. Fill in the missing letter in each spelling demon. Use a dictionary to check your answers.

EXAMPLE: adje_c_tive

1. inflamm__ble
2. benefi__ial
3. calend__r
4. controver__ial
5. extraordin__ry
6. desp__rate
7. an__cdote
8. audi__nce
9. subst__tute
10. prote__n
11. a__rosol
12. elig__ble
13. twel__th
14. pig__on
15. s__issors
16. h__pnotic
17. pre__ision
18. emerg__ncy
19. env__lope
20. exist__nce

Copyright © by Prentice-Hall, Inc.

NAME _____ CLASS _____ DATE _____

27.1 Techniques for Improving Spelling

Studying Problem Words
Use a dictionary to correct spelling errors and record problem words in a personal spelling list.

MEMORIZING THE SPELLING OF PROBLEM WORDS
1. Observe each word on your list carefully, noticing the arrangement of letters. 2. Pronounce the word to yourself, making sure to pronounce each syllable. 3. Write each word and then check to see that you have spelled it correctly. 4. Review your list until you have mastered each word.

Developing Memory Aids
Use memory aids to improve your spelling.

Diagnosing Problem Areas
Analyze your spelling errors to determine your areas of weakness and then study the rules that will help you.

Setting Goals for Improvement
Record all problem words on a personal spelling list and memorize them a few at a time.

EXERCISE A: Creating a Personal Spelling List. Correct the spelling of each misspelled word. Then write a hint for remembering the correct spelling.

EXAMPLE: nusance   _nuisance_   _A nuisance is annoying._

1. arguement _____ _____
2. tomatos _____ _____
3. analize _____ _____
4. jornal _____ _____
5. nabor _____ _____
6. dinning room _____ _____
7. behavor _____ _____
8. dispair _____ _____
9. lightening _____ _____
10. acomodate _____ _____

EXERCISE B: Creating Memory Aids. Underline a familiar word within each larger word listed below. Then use both the smaller word and the larger word in a sentence that will help you remember the spelling demon.

EXAMPLE: extra<u>ordinary</u>   _An extra<u>ordinary</u> person is not <u>ordinary</u>._

1. temperament _____
2. symmetrical _____
3. recommend _____
4. correspondence _____
5. contemporary _____

NAME _____ CLASS _____ DATE _____

27.2 A Catalog of Spelling Rules

Plurals

Add -s or -es to form the plural of most nouns.

FORMING PLURALS OF NOUNS		
Noun Ending	**Rule**	**Examples**
s, x, z, sh, ch	Add -es	dresses, taxes, waltzes, leashes, bunches
o preceded by a consonant	Add -es	tomatoes (Exception: musical terms)
o preceded by a vowel	Add -s	portfolios, rodeos
y preceded by a consonant	Change y to i and add -es	juries, pennies
y preceded by a vowel	Just add -s	displays, turkeys
f, ff, fe	Add -s	roofs, chiefs, puffs (Exception: wives, loaves)

EXERCISE A: Making Words Plural. Write the plural form of each word listed below. Use a dictionary to check your spelling.

EXAMPLE: army _____armies_____

1. diary _____
2. branch _____
3. tornado _____
4. highway _____
5. cameo _____
6. crisis _____
7. goose _____
8. hoof _____
9. city _____
10. hero _____
11. calf _____
12. cuff _____
13. address _____
14. mix _____
15. mosquito _____
16. pony _____
17. leaf _____
18. analysis _____
19. alto _____
20. fly _____

EXERCISE B: More Work with Plurals. In each blank, fill in the plural for the word in parentheses.

EXAMPLE: The ___sheep___ were grazing in the field. (sheep)

1. Most husbands get along with their _____ quite well. (mother-in-law)
2. Sue and Jack spent the afternoon picking _____. (blueberry)
3. The company has had three _____ in the past ten years. (chief executive officer)
4. Many _____ were damaged by the storm. (tree)
5. Mary saw several _____ in her backyard this morning. (deer)
6. There are two _____ at the university. (poet-in-residence)
7. Several _____ witnessed the crime. (passer-by)
8. The Smiths are going to Texas for the _____. (holiday)
9. The _____ gathered to discuss intertribal relations. (chief)
10. Ronald caught a dozen _____ today. (trout)

27.2 A Catalog of Spelling Rules

Prefixes and Suffixes

When a prefix is added to a word, the spelling of the root word remains the same. Before adding a suffix, notice the last letters of the root and the first letter of the suffix.

ADDING PREFIXES	
With No Change	**With Prefix Change**
mis + place = misplace semi + soft = semisoft un + just = unjust	ad + cord = accord in + regular = irregular ob + pose = oppose

ADDING SUFFIXES	
With No Change	**With Change**
care + ful = careful destroy + er = destroyer retire + ment = retirement pour + ing = pouring	defense + ive = defensive map + ing = mapping plenty + ful = plentiful transmit + ed = transmitted

EXERCISE A: Spelling Words with Prefixes. Combine each of the following roots with one of the prefixes below. You may have to change the spelling of the prefix. Some roots can combine with more than one prefix.

ad-, com-, in-, pre-, post-, sub-, semi-, trans-, un-

EXAMPLE: -sweet ____semisweet____

1. -record _____
2. -familiar _____
3. -circle _____
4. -possible _____
5. -port _____
6. -date _____
7. -firm _____
8. -vocate _____
9. -pose _____
10. -aware _____

EXERCISE B: Spelling Words with Suffixes. Write the new word form by combining each of the following words and suffixes.

EXAMPLE: improve + ing ____improving____

1. empty + ed _____
2. taste + ful _____
3. cure + able _____
4. admit + ance _____
5. dive + er _____
6. display + ed _____
7. candid + ness _____
8. beat + en _____
9. observe + ance _____
10. fancy + ful _____

27.2 A Catalog of Spelling Rules

ie and ei Words

According to a well-known rule, write *i* before *e* except after *c* or when sounded like *a* in *neighbor* and *weigh*. There are a number of exceptions to this rule.

EXCEPTIONS TO THE *ie* AND *ei* RULE	
***ei* Exceptions**	***ie* Exceptions**
either leisure sheik foreign neither their height seize weird	(When *c* is pronounced *sh*) ancient efficient conscience sufficient

Words Ending in -cede, -ceed, and -sede.

Memorize the spellings of words that end in *-cede*, *-ceed*, *-sede*.

Words Ending in *-cede*	Words Ending in *-ceed*	Words Ending in *-sede*
accede precede concede recede intercede secede	exceed proceed succeed	supersede

EXERCISE A: Spelling *ie* and *ei* Words. Complete each numbered word by inserting *ie* or *ei*. Use a dictionary to check your spelling.

EXAMPLE: N*e i*ther of us bel*i e*ved him.

An (1) effic___ ___ncy expert (2) conc___ ___ved of a plan to help several workers increase (3) th___ ___r productivity. "First," he said, "you must remove this (4) anc___ ___nt equipment from your office. It does not (5) suffic___ ___ntly meet your needs. Secondly, you must (6) s___ ___ze every moment (7) ___ ___ther to work or to plan future projects. In good (8) consc___ ___nce I cannot recommend taking a (9) l___ ___surely attitude. There is too much (10) for___ ___gn competition."

EXERCISE B: Spelling Words Ending in -cede, -ceed, and -sede. Fill in the correct letters in the spaces below.

EXAMPLE: Mr. Jones was forced to inter___*cede*___ in the dispute.

1. Ann's parents are confident that she will suc_____ in whatever profession she chooses.
2. The rash on Ron's leg is starting to re_____.
3. The president refused to ac_____ to the terrorists' demands.
4. The general manager said that his latest order super_____s all of his previous orders.
5. Several countries voted to se_____ from the alliance.
6. No one was willing to inter_____ when a fight broke out between two football players.
7. We must pro_____ with extreme caution.
8. Mrs. Jackson was certain that the cost of the repairs would ex_____ the estimate.
9. A group of security guards pre_____ed the president in the procession.
10. The debater refused to con_____ a point to his opponent.

27.2 A Catalog of Spelling Rules

Other Confusing Endings
Learn to distinguish between confusing groups of suffixes.

CONFUSING SUFFIXES				
-able	*-ible*	*-ance*	*-ence*	*-efy*
acceptable	convertible	abundance	coincidence	liquefy
believable	eligible	acquaintance	excellence	putrefy
irritable	permissible	assistance	lenience	rarefy
predictable	reversible	guidance	patience	stupefy
-ary	*-ery*	*-cy*	*-sy*	*-ify*
imaginary	cemetery	efficiency	courtesy	beautify
military	millinery	dependency	embassy	clarify
secondary	scenery	deficiency	fantasy	notify
vocabulary	stationery	fluency	hypocrisy	mollify
-eous	*-ious*	*-sion*	*-tion*	
beauteous	anxious	abrasion	alteration	
erroneous	contagious	aggression	appreciation	
miscellaneous	ingenious	confusion	contradiction	
simultaneous	fictitious	illusion	justification	

EXERCISE A: Spelling Suffixes Correctly. Fill in the missing letters in each of the words below.

EXAMPLE: predict__a__ble

1. acquaint___nce
2. permiss___ble
3. liqu___fy
4. imagin___ry
5. guid___nce
6. simpl___fy
7. irrit___ble
8. accept___ble
9. contradic_____n
10. miscellan_____s
11. putr___fy
12. convert___ble
13. anx_____s
14. scen___ry
15. confus_____n
16. coincid___nce
17. altera_____n
18. fictit_____s
19. beaut_____s
20. court_____y

EXERCISE B: Recognizing Correct Spellings. Circle the correctly spelled word in each pair of words in parentheses.

EXAMPLE: That story is not entirely (believable, believible).

1. Karen is (eligable, eligible) to be in the semifinals.
2. I am trying to improve my (vocabulary, vocabulery).
3. The librarian offered me some (assistance, assistence).
4. The ambassador left the (embascy, embassy) at noon.
5. His statement was (erroneous, erronious).
6. Mrs. Flynn has a great deal of (patiance, patience) with her class.
7. Is the measles a (contagious, contageous) disease?
8. I sent a letter expressing my (appreciation, appreciasion).
9. What an (ingeneous, ingenious) device!
10. I need some (stationary, stationery) with our school letterhead.

NAME _____ CLASS _____ DATE _____

28.1 Evaluating Your Study Habits

Developing a Study Plan

Develop a study plan to manage your time most efficiently. Your study plan should include setting up a study area, establishing a study schedule, and using an assignment book.

PLANNING AN ASSIGNMENT BOOK

1. Divide your assignment book pages into four columns, using one column for the subject, one for a description of the assignment, one for the due date, and one for a check when the assignment is completed.
2. Record short-term assignments such as homework.
3. Record long-term assignments such as a research paper, dividing the assignment into short-term goals.

Setting Goals

Set long- and short-term goals to improve your general study habits.

SETTING LONG- AND SHORT-TERM GOALS

Long-term Goal: To set up a study area

Short-term Goals	Timetable	Comments
To choose an area that is well lighted and free of distractions	1 week (by April 7)	Successfully completed
To equip the study area with all the necessary materials	2 weeks (by April 14)	Successfully completed
To use the study area for all school work, including reading and studying for tests	1 month (by April 28)	Need to work on completing reading assignments while sitting at a desk

---

EXERCISE A: Setting Up a Study Schedule. Use the spaces provided below to make up a study schedule that suits your personal needs. Be sure to include at least two hours of study time.

Time	Activity
8:00–3:00	School
_____	_____
_____	_____
_____	_____
_____	_____

EXERCISE B: Setting Goals for Study Skills. Select one study skill that you want to master. Then complete the activities below.

1. Set a long-term goal. _____
2. Set a short-term goal. _____
3. Set a second short-term goal. _____
4. Set a third short-term goal. _____
5. Now set a timetable for your short-term goals. _____

Copyright © by Prentice-Hall, Inc.

NAME _____ CLASS _____ DATE _____

28.2 Methods of Taking Notes

Making Outlines

Organize your notes by using one of three types of outlines: modified outlines, formal outlines, or free-form outlines.

TYPES OF OUTLINES	
Type	**Purpose**
Modified	For taking notes while listening or reading
Formal	For arranging ideas while preparing major written or oral assignments
Free-Form	For taking notes from loosely organized material

Writing Summaries

Use summaries to take notes when you need to remember only the main ideas.

WRITING SUMMARIES
1. Listen or read for main ideas.
2. Write down the main idea using your own words.
3. Shape these main ideas into sentences.
4. Write a summary in paragraph form.

Developing a Personal Shorthand

Develop a personal shorthand for efficient note-taking.

EXERCISE A: Making a Modified Outline. Listen to a radio or TV interview or a segment of a documentary. Or listen to a recording of a speech. Use the questions below to prepare a modified outline.

1. Who is the source of the information? _____
2. When and where was the information presented? _____
3. What is the main idea? _____
4. What are the supporting ideas? _____
   _____
5. On a separate piece of paper, write the main idea and supporting ideas in modified outline form.

EXERCISE B: Writing a Summary. Read a newspaper or magazine article. Use the questions below to plan a summary of your article.

1. What is the title of the article and who wrote it? _____
2. Where and when was it published? _____
3. What is the main idea of the article? _____
   _____
4. What are the supporting ideas? _____
   _____
5. On a separate piece of paper, write the main idea and supporting ideas in summary form.

NAME _____ CLASS _____ DATE _____

29.1 Forms of Reasoning

Using Fact and Opinion
Analyze material first to decide if it is reliable.

DISTINGUISHING BETWEEN FACTS AND OPINIONS	
Statements of Fact	Objective statements that can be verified
Statements of Opinion	Subjective statements that cannot be verified but must be supported with related facts before being accepted as valid.

Using Valid Reasoning
Think logically to draw valid conclusions.

FORMS OF REASONING		
Form	Valid Use	Invalid Use
Inductive Reasoning	A generalization that holds true in a large number of cases or is supported by evidence	A generalization that is made without accounting for exceptions
Deductive Reasoning	The application of a general statement that is assumed to be true to specific cases	A restatement of the general statement that fails to include supporting facts or evidence
Cause and Effect	A sequence in which something is caused by one or more events that occurred before it	A sequence in which the first event did not cause the second event
Analogy	A comparison between two different objects or events that are similar in some important way	A comparison that fails to account for essential dissimilarities

EXERCISE A: Distinguishing Between Facts and Opinions. Identify each of the following statements as a *fact* or an *opinion*.

EXAMPLE: Polar bears are larger than penguins. ___fact___

1. Hank Aaron was the greatest baseball player of all time. _____
2. Gold is more valuable than silver. _____
3. The weather in California is better than the weather in Maine. _____
4. The United States won the most gold medals in the 1984 Olympics. _____
5. *Hamlet* is Shakespeare's finest play. _____

EXERCISE B: Analyzing Forms of Reasoning. Identify the form of reasoning in each of the following statements as *inductive reasoning, deductive reasoning, cause and effect,* or *analogy*. Then, for each case, tell whether the conclusion drawn is valid or invalid.

EXAMPLE: John got sick because he stayed up until 2:00 last night.
___cause and effect___   ___invalid___

1. Because of the performer's popularity, the concert was sold out.

2. Days pass by like grains of sand swept away by the changing tides.

3. Jack rides a bicycle during the summer. Jack is a ski racer. Therefore, all ski racers ride bicycles during the summer.

4. All surfers are good swimmers. Sue is a surfer. Therefore, Sue is a good swimmer.

29.2 Language and Thinking

Uses of Language
Learn to identify different uses of language.

USES OF LANGUAGE	
Denotation	The *denotation* of a word is its literal or exact meaning.
Connotation	The *connotation* of a word is its suggested or implied meaning.
Irony	*Irony* occurs when the intended meaning of a statement is opposite to the literal meaning.
Jargon	*Jargon* is specialized and technical language that is important in certain technical areas, professions, and hobbies.
Euphemism	A *euphemism* is a word or phrase used in place of others that are considered unpleasant or offensive.

EXERCISE A: Analyzing the Uses of Language. Identify each of the items below as an example of *denotation, connotation, irony, jargon,* or *euphemism.*

EXAMPLE: Her handwriting is so neat that it took me three hours to decipher her note. __irony__

1. Sally Gibson owns a ranch in Texas. _____
2. When he sensed that the opposing team's linebackers were going to blitz, the quarterback called an audible. _____
3. The boxer laid his opponent to rest with a powerful right hook. _____
4. Sally crept down the road with the grace of a snail. _____
5. Lucinda's Saint Bernard is so petite that he takes up the entire back seat of her car. _____
6. Billy is so good at giving directions that everyone that he invited to his party got lost on their way to his house. _____
7. The politician smiled deceitfully as he assured the crowd that his intentions were good. _____
8. Sally believes that all of her husband's ailments are psychosomatic, resulting from a neurotic disorder. _____
9. Walter walked slowly down the street past the grocery store and the gas station. _____
10. The general manager called Gertrude into his office and informed her that she wouldn't have to worry about getting up for work any more. _____

EXERCISE B: More Work with the Uses of Language. Follow the directions in Exercise A.

1. The band played for three hours at last night's concert. _____
2. His advice was so valuable that we chose to totally disregard it. _____
3. Alice rarely smiles because of her malocclusion. _____
4. The quarterback displayed his total lack of competence, fumbling the football three times in the first quarter. _____
5. When he and his wife separated, William told his wife that he would attempt to relieve her of the burden of caring for their son by suing for custody of the child. _____

NAME _____ CLASS _____ DATE _____

30.1 Reading Skills

Reading Textbooks

Use textbook reading and study aids to help you understand and remember what you read.

USING THE SQ4R METHOD	
Survey	Preview the material you are going to read.
Question	Turn each heading into a question.
Read	Answer the questions you have posed.
Recite	Orally recall the questions and answers.
Record	Take notes to further reinforce information
Review	Review the material on a regular basis.

Varying Your Reading Style

Change your reading style whenever your purpose in reading changes.

TYPES OF READING STYLES		
Style	Definition	Purpose
Phrase reading	Reading groups of words in order to understand all the material	For studying, solving problems, and following directions
Skimming	Skipping words in order to read rapidly and get a quick overview	For previewing, reviewing, and locating information
Scanning	Reading in order to locate a particular piece of information	For researching, reviewing, and finding information

EXERCISE A: Using the SQ4R Method. Choose a chapter in one of your textbooks to use in completing the work below.

1. List the chapter headings and subtitles. _____
_____

2. Turn two of these headings into questions. _____
_____
_____

3. Read the chapter. Then answer the questions you wrote in #2. _____
_____
_____

4. List the main ideas contained in the chapter. _____
_____

5. List the major details used to support one of these ideas. _____
_____
_____

EXERCISE B: Varying Your Reading Style. Skim through a chapter in one of your textbooks and write a summary. Then read through the chapter again using the phrase reading method and write a modified outline on separate paper.

NAME _____ CLASS _____ DATE _____

30.1 Reading Skills

Reading Critically

Read critically in order to question, analyze, and evaluate what you read.

SKILLS FOR READING CRITICALLY
1. *Suspend judgment* about the meaning of what you read until you can gather enough facts to make an informed decision. 2. *Ask questions* in order to determine the meaning of what you read. 3. *Test the questions* about meaning using methods of logic and reasoned thinking. 4. *Evaluate* the meaning of what you read based on reasoned thinking and personal experience.

EXERCISE A: Asking Critical-Reading Questions. Find a newspaper or magazine article that deals with a controversial issue. Then read the article critically to answer the questions below.

1. What audience is the author addressing? _____
2. What is the author's purpose in writing the article? _____
3. Does the author make use of connotation, or suggested meanings of words, to make the reader feel a certain way? If so, give an example. _____
_____
4. Does the author distinguish between facts and opinions? _____
5. Are the author's opinions supported by facts? Support your answer. _____
_____
6. Does the author use irony or understatement to imply meaning different from the one stated and expect you to understand the intended meaning? Support your answer. _____
_____
7. Does the author present ideas in a reasoned, logical manner? Support your answer. _____
_____
8. Are the author's conclusions supported by evidence? Support your answer.
_____
9. Do the author's conclusions follow from the facts being presented? Support your answer. _____
_____
10. Is emotion rather than reason being used to persuade the reader? Support your answer. _____
_____

EXERCISE B: More Work with Critical Reading. Using the article you read for Exercise A, answer the questions below.

1. Does the author accomplish his or her purpose? If so, how? _____
_____
2. Does the author have something of value to say? Support your answer. _____
_____
3. What are the implications of the author's ideas? _____
_____
4. Do the author's ideas increase your understanding? If so, how? _____
_____
5. Do the author's ideas change your views on the issue being discussed? If so, how? _____
_____

NAME _____ CLASS _____ DATE _____

30.2 Standardized Tests

Taking Standardized Tests
Prepare for standardized tests by studying consistently and reading widely.

Answering Vocabulary Questions
Learn the types of vocabulary questions and the strategies for answering them.

ANSWERING VOCABULARY QUESTIONS	
Antonym Questions	Look for a word among the answer choices that is as opposite from the given word as possible and is the same part of speech.
Analogy Questions	Define both words in the initial pair and define the relationship between these two words, making sure that you keep the pair of words in the order given.
Sentence Completion Questions	Read the sentence and try to fill in the blank(s) before looking at the choices, and use signal words to predict the correct answer.

EXERCISE A: Answering Sentence Completion Questions. Circle the word that best completes each of the following sentences.

EXAMPLE: Several _____ spoke about the wildlife of the area.
(a) zoophytes (b) constables (c) (zoologists) (d) wildcats (e) audience

1. Lee has acquired his fine skills through years of _____ training.
   (a) archaic (b) effortless (c) infrequent (d) arduous (e) leisurely

2. Before the investigation, we could only _____ as to the causes.
   (a) facilitate (b) speculate (c) certify (d) spectacle (e) suffice

3. An eponym is a person's name that a word is later _____ from, as Jules Leotard, the originator of a one-piece garment worn by dancers.
   (a) derived (b) connoted (c) personified (d) copied (e) specified

4. The companies decided to _____ rather than operate separately.
   (a) commit (b) constrain (c) consolidate (d) fragment (e) persuade

EXERCISE B: Answering Analogy Questions. Circle the terms that best complete each analogy.

EXAMPLE: bicycle:pedal::
   (a) handle:briefcase (b) (typewriter:key) (c) book:shelf
   (d) diamond:jewelry (e) pedal:handlebar

1. car:dashboard::
   (a) wing:airplane (b) string:kite (c) curtain:stage (d) pencil:paper
   (e) boat:deck

2. freeze:frozen::
   (a) wear:worn (b) do:doing (c) eat:ate (d) sit:set (e) cold:colder

3. dim:faint::
   (a) tempting:uninviting (b) worthy:belief (c) practical:idea
   (d) rare:unusual (e) light:bolt

4. sculptor:chisel::
   (a) paint:artist (b) lawyer:jury (c) stethoscope:instrument
   (d) conductor:baton (e) carpenter:bookcase

Copyright © by Prentice-Hall, Inc.

NAME _____ CLASS _____ DATE _____

30.2 Standardized Tests

Answering Reading Comprehension Questions
Learn to identify and answer the six types of reading comprehension questions.

| ANSWERING READING COMPREHENSION QUESTIONS ||
Question	Strategy
Main Idea	Determine what the entire selection is about.
Detail	Scan the passage to find the answer.
Inference	Make a generalization based on specific facts.
Definition	Make use of context clues.
Tone/Purpose	Look at the author's choice of words.
Form	Look at the organizational pattern.

EXERCISE A: Answering Reading Comprehension Questions. Read the selection below. Then circle the answers to the questions that follow.

Mark Twain once wrote that a cauliflower is merely a "cabbage with a college education." What he meant was that its appearance is more polished and refined than the ordinary cabbage to which it is related. But a college education should do more than polish the outer surface and turn us into "cauliflowers." A college should be a place where students learn to explore ideas. This is accomplished through reading, discussing, experimenting, and writing. College should be a place where students learn traditional ways of viewing the world and formulate new paradigms which yield even greater insights into the human experience. With that kind of training, a student will be truly "cultivated."

1. A good title for this selection is
   (a) Cauliflower (b) A True College Education (c) Preparing for the Future (d) Who Needs College? (e) How to Learn
2. To what did Mark Twain compare a cauliflower?
   (a) cabbage (b) college (c) experience (e) appearance
3. The author thinks that students need to be
   (a) polished (b) models (c) active learners (d) scientific (e) passive
4. The word *paradigms* in the ninth sentence means
   (a) parallels (b) lists (c) experiences (d) traditions (e) models
5. The writer's feelings about college can be termed
   (a) strong (b) indifferent (c) angry (d) uncertain (e) surprised

EXERCISE B: More Work with Reading Comprehension. Follow the directions in Exercise A.

Not only has television played a major role in the growth of the popularity of professional sports over the past several decades, but it has also played a primary role in the escalation of players' salaries. In recent years, players' salaries have increased dramatically. To a great extent this is due to the revenues generated by television coverage of professional sports. Networks pay millions of dollars to professional leagues for the right to televise large numbers of games. Realizing this, players have demanded radical increases in salary and the average incomes of professional athletes have skyrocketed.

1. The author's central concern is
   (a) football (b) sports (c) popularity (d) the rise in salaries in professional sports (e) golf
2. In recent years, players' salaries have
   (a) increased slightly (b) decreased slightly (c) stayed the same (d) increased greatly (e) decreased greatly
3. Television has affected players' salaries
   (a) positively (b) radically (c) indirectly (d) negatively (e) in no way
4. The author's purpose is to
   (a) criticize (b) inform (c) ridicule (d) describe (e) entertain

NAME _____ CLASS _____ DATE _____

30.2 Standardized Tests

Tests of Standard Written English
Learn to identify the grammar, usage, and mechanics for standard written English.

> **TAKING STANDARD WRITTEN-EXPRESSION TESTS**
> 1. Read a sentence or passage through twice before making any decisions about answers.
> 2. Look for errors according to difficulty.
> 3. Identify the subject and predicate of each sentence to help you find errors in usage, redundancy, and relevance.

EXERCISE A: Answering Usage Questions. The sentences below contain errors in grammar, usage, word choice, and idiom. Parts of the sentences are underlined and lettered. Decide which underlined part contains the error and circle its letter, or circle (e) if the sentence is correct. No sentence contains more than one error.

EXAMPLE: (a) Next (b) Tuesday's test ((c)) was (d) difficult. (e) No error

1. Jim (a) says that his favorite activities are (b) sleeping, (c) eating, and (d) to watch television. (e) No error
2. Wendy (a) waited in line for ten hours (b) to buy tickets to the Rolling Stones' concert (c) because she really (d) hates their music. (e) No error
3. (a) When he (b) was younger, Horace (c) will be an (d) exceptional soccer player. (e) No error
4. Suzy (a) can throw a frisbee (b) a great deal (c) further than Ellen (d) can. (e) No error.
5. Ron (a) told me that he (b) is (c) already for (d) today's math quiz. (e) No error.

EXERCISE B: Answering Sentence Completion Questions. The sentences below contain errors in sentence construction, word choice, and punctuation. Select the lettered answer that contains the best version of the underlined section. Answer (a) repeats the original underlined section exactly. If the sentence is correct as it stands, select (a).

EXAMPLE: Whom thought of going to the beach today?
(a) Whom (b) Who's ((c)) Who (d) Whoever (e) Whose

1. Because he studied hard, Jackson failed the test.
   (a) Because he studied hard (b) Even though he studied hard (c) Since he studied hard (d) Even though he did not study (e) Whenever he studies
2. Katie preceded down the road in spite of the fact that it was closed.
   (a) preceded down (b) preceded through (c) proceeded down (d) proceeded on (e) receded down
3. It was a meticulous game for the home team.
   (a) meticulous (b) crucial (c) precarious (d) urgent (e) faultfinding
4. After winning the game the team celebrated by going out to dinner.
   (a) After winning the game the (b) After, winning the game, the (c) After playing the game the (d) After winning the game, the (e) After losing the game the
5. Ronald did extremely well on last week's English test.
   (a) did extremely well (b) did very good (c) will do well (d) will do good (e) would have passed

Copyright © by Prentice-Hall, Inc.

165

NAME _____ CLASS _____ DATE _____

31.1 Library Skills

Planning Your Research

To begin your research, gather basic information about your topic.

BASIC INFORMATION ABOUT A RESEARCH TOPIC	
Information	Example
1. A clear statement of the topic	acid rain
2. A more general subject area	pollution
3. Synonyms that describe your topic	atmospheric acidity
4. Related subjects	fossil fuels, air quality
5. Time period involved	present
6. Geographical area involved	U.S., Canada

Using the Card Catalog

Use the card catalog to find out information about a library's books and other materials.

Going from Catalog to Shelf

Use the catalog card location symbol to locate materials on library shelves.

Item	Method of Finding on the Shelf
Nonfiction	Use a call number.
Fiction	Find the fiction section and then look for the author's last name.
Biography	Find the biography section and then look for the subject's last name.
Reference Book	Find the reference section and then use the call numbers.

EXERCISE A: Gathering Basic Information About a Research Topic. Select a research topic that interests you. Then supply the following information about your topic.

1. A clear statement of your topic _____
2. A more general subject area your topic could be listed under _____
3. Synonyms for your topic _____
4. Related subjects _____
5. The time period and geographical period involved _____

EXERCISE B: Locating Fiction. Number the following works of fiction in the order in which you would find them on the library shelves.

1. William Faulkner, *Sanctuary* ___
2. John Updike, *Rabbit Run* ___
3. Toni Morrison, *Tar Baby* ___
4. Joyce Carol Oates, *Expensive Loves* ___
5. William Faulkner, *The Wild Palms* ___
6. Jane Austen, *Pride and Prejudice* ___
7. John Updike, *Rabbit Redux* ___
8. John Updike, *Rabbit Is Rich* ___
9. Toni Morrison, *Sula* ___
10. Joyce Carol Oates, *Them* ___

NAME _____ CLASS _____ DATE _____

31.2 Reference Skills

General Reference Books

Use general reference books to check basic facts or explore the range of a topic.

General Reference Books	What They Contain
Encyclopedias	Basic information about almost all general topics
Almanacs	Facts and statistics on a wide range of subjects, including sports, government, and famous people
Atlases	Current or historical maps, often showing more than just political or geographical details
Gazetteers	Facts about places around the world

Specialized Reference Books

Use specialized reference books to find in-depth information about a particular field.

Periodicals and Pamphlets

Use periodicals and pamphlets to find current, concise information.

Other Ways of Obtaining Reference Materials

For information unavailable in your library, consult national and local organizations, whose addresses may be obtained in your library.

EXERCISE A: Using General Reference Books. Use encyclopedias, almanacs, atlases, and gazetteers to find the information requested below. Give the information and the source of information.

EXAMPLE: The deepest lake in the United States
    Crater Lake, Oregon, World Almanac & Book of Facts, 1984

1. Two buildings designed by Frank Lloyd Wright _____
2. The year Kansas became a state _____
3. The site of the 1976 Olympic Games _____
4. The latitude and longitude of Nome, Alaska _____
5. Two museums that are part of the Smithsonian Institution _____
6. The rainiest spot in the U.S. _____
7. Three American states that share a border with Canada _____
8. The Vice President under Franklin D. Roosevelt during his last term _____
9. The highest point of elevation on the continent of Australia _____
10. The countries that border Bolivia _____

EXERCISE B: Using *The Readers' Guide*. Use *The Readers' Guide* entry below to answer the questions that follow.

Acid Rain: unproved threat or deadly fact? C. E. Riemer and J. W. Miller. il *Good Housekeep* 198:236 Je '84

EXAMPLE: Subject heading under which article is found   _Acid Rain_
1. Title of the article _____
2. Authors _____
3. Title of the magazine _____
4. Volume and page numbers _____
5. Date of Issue _____

31.3 Dictionary Skills

Recognizing Kinds of General Dictionaries
Use a dictionary that suits your needs. Use an unabridged dictionary when you need very specific definitions and extremely detailed information about words. Use an abridged dictionary for everyday use.

Knowing What Dictionaries Contain
Learn to recognize and use the various features of your own dictionary.

FEATURES FOUND IN ABRIDGED DICTIONARIES	
Front Matter	Inflected Forms
Back Matter	Etymologies
Main Entries	Definitions
Preferred and Variant Spellings	Usage and Field Labels
Syllabification	Idioms
Pronunciation	Derived Words and Run-on Entries
Part-of-Speech Labels	Synonymies

EXERCISE A: Alphabetizing Entry Words. Number the following words in the order in which you would find them in the dictionary.

____ a. friendly
____ b. friendship
____ c. friary
____ d. friction drive
____ e. friction
____ f. fricassee
____ g. friction layer
____ h. fried cake
____ i. friended
____ j. fried

EXERCISE B: Using a Dictionary. Consult an abridged dictionary to answer the following questions.

EXAMPLE: What is the pronunciation of *annihilate*? ____ ə nī ´ə lāt

1. Is *litre* a preferred or variant spelling? _____
2. What is the pronunciation of *metabolic*? _____
3. As which parts of speech can the word *goad* be used? _____
4. What is the past participle of the verb *occur*? _____
5. What is the definition of the noun *rime*? _____
6. What is the origin of the word *museum*? _____
7. What field label do you find with the word *preachy*? _____
8. What is one word derived from *harmless*? _____
9. What is the meaning of the idiom *to read out of*? _____
10. What are the differences between the synonyms *pale, pallid,* and *ashen*? _____

NAME _____ CLASS _____ DATE _____

32.1 Getting a Job

Writing a Résumé

Keep an updated résumé ready to send to potential employers.

ELEMENTS TO INCLUDE IN YOUR RÉSUMÉ
1. *The Heading:* your name, address, and telephone number
2. *Position Desired:* the type of work you would like
3. *Education:* your educational background
4. *Interests:* interests that could be helpful in your career
5. *Activities:* clubs and organizations you belong to
6. *References:* names, addresses, and telephone numbers of people who are familiar with your work

Reading Classified Want Ads

Become familiar with the abbreviations used in classified want ads.

ABBREVIATIONS USED IN CLASSIFIED WANT ADS					
asst	assistant	lrn	learn	O/T	overtime
exp'd	experienced	mfr	manufacturer	reg	registered
int'l	international	oppty	opportunity	sal	salary
				w/, w/o	with, without

Filling Out a Job Application

Fill out job applications carefully. Keep two objectives in mind.

EXERCISE A: Understanding Classified Want Ads. Rewrite the following classified ads, giving the full form for each abbreviation used.

EXAMPLE: MEDICAL SECY F/T Exp. req'd. knwl. insurance forms nec., lite typing, pleasant manner. Sal open 279-8016.
  MEDICAL SECRETARY, full time. Experience required. Knowledge of insurance forms necessary. Light typing and pleasant manner. Salary open. Call 279-8016.

1. PHARMACISTS. Excel oppty for reg Pharm, offering incentives + sal for FT pos. P/T pos also avail.

2. DRIVER w/ van or stat wag-Full time, $450/wk possible.

3. COSMETICS. Prestigious cosmetic co. needs exp'd demonstrators for maj dept stores in NY/NJ/CT. Call for interview Mon aft.

4. CARPENTER MECHANIC. Exp in gen'l construction. Window & door installation a must. Driver's lic nec. Sal commens w/ exp.

EXERCISE B: Planning a Résumé. Look through the classified want ads in your local newspaper. Find a job you are qualified to apply for. Then write a résumé you could send if you were applying for that job. Include the parts listed in the chart above. Emphasize your particular qualifications for the job.

NAME _____ CLASS _____ DATE _____

32.2 Next Steps

Preparing for a Job Interview

Prepare for a job interview by finding out about the job and reviewing your résumé.

PREPARING FOR AN INTERVIEW
1. Learn as much as you can about the job and the employer.
2. Choose appropriate clothing.
3. Review your résumé.
4. Be prepared to ask questions about the job.

Interviewing for a Job

Present a positive image to a potential employer.

EXERCISE A: Preparing for an Interview. Select a job that you would like to apply for. Then, in the spaces provided below, prepare a list of ten questions that you could ask a job interviewer. Include questions about responsibilities, employee benefits, and possible promotions.

1. _____
2. _____
3. _____
4. _____
5. _____
6. _____
7. _____
8. _____
9. _____
10. _____

EXERCISE B: Answering an Interviewer's Questions. Using the job that you selected in Exercise A, answer the questions below.

1. Why are you interested in the job you are applying for? _____
_____
_____

2. What skills would you bring to this job? _____
_____
_____
_____

3. What are your career goals? _____
_____
_____

4. What were your responsibilities in your last job? _____
_____
_____

5. What are your greatest strengths? _____
_____

NAME _____ CLASS _____ DATE _____

33.1 Interviews

Conducting an Interview

Conducting an interview requires careful preparation, management, and follow-up.

CONDUCTING AN INTERVIEW
1. Bring a paper and pencil and/or tape recorder to record the interviewee's responses.
2. Arrive promptly and greet the interviewee by introducing yourself and explaining the purpose of the interview.
3. Keep the conversation related to the interview topic.
4. End the interview when your questions have been answered and you have the information you need.

EXERCISE A: Preparing to Conduct an Interview. Prepare to conduct an interview by completing the work below.

1. What is your topic? _____
2. Whom are you interviewing? _____
3. What is the purpose of your interview? _____
   _____
4. Briefly summarize the interviewee's background and expertise. _____
   _____
5. Write six questions that you will ask the interviewee. _____
   _____
   _____
   _____
   _____
   _____

EXERCISE B: Conducting an Interview. Using the work you completed in Exercise A, conduct an interview to gather information about your topic. Use the space provided below to record the interviewee's responses.

_____
_____
_____
_____
_____
_____
_____
_____
_____
_____
_____
_____
_____
_____

Copyright © by Prentice-Hall, Inc.

NAME _____ CLASS _____ DATE _____

33.2 Group Discussion and Parliamentary Procedure

Recognizing Different Kinds of Group Discussions

A group discussion is formed to achieve a specific common goal.

KINDS OF GROUP DISCUSSIONS	
Round-table Discussion Group	A group formed in order to share information
Committee	A small group of a larger organization formed to discuss specific ideas
Panel	A group of several informed people who hold a discussion with an audience present
Symposium	A group in which each member gives a formal speech on one aspect of a topic with an audience present

Holding a Group Discussion

A group discussion should focus on a timely, interesting topic that the members are involved with and prepared to discuss.

PLANNING A GROUP DISCUSSION
1. Hold a prediscussion meeting to determine the discussion topic.
2. Define the topic precisely and phrase it as a question.
3. Make an outline of points to be discussed, including a history of the problem, alternatives or solutions, and possible action to be taken.
4. Research the topic.

EXERCISE A: Recognizing Different Kinds of Group Discussions. Identify the kinds of group discussions referred to in each item below.

EXAMPLE: A group of doctors discuss the dangers of cigarette smoking before a group of high school students. ___*panel*___

1. Several members of a country club hold an informal meeting to discuss an upcoming social function. _____
2. A painter, a sculptor, and a potter talk about their respective crafts before the members of an art class. _____
3. A group of executives from a large corporation discuss the possibility of purchasing a publishing company. _____
4. Several politicians discuss the problem of pollution before a group of taxpayers. _____
5. Four journalists discuss the effect of television on journalism before a group of interested spectators. _____

EXERCISE B: Planning a Group Discussion. Complete the activities below.

1. Choose a topic. _____
2. Define the topic precisely. _____
   _____
3. Phrase the topic as a question. _____
4. On a separate sheet of paper, make an outline of points to be discussed.
5. List two sources that you will use in researching your topic. _____
   _____

172   Copyright © by Prentice-Hall, Inc.

NAME _____ CLASS _____ DATE _____

33.2 Group Discussion and Parliamentary Procedure

Using Parliamentary Procedure

Parliamentary procedure guarantees that the rights of the majority and minority are respected and that a meeting is conducted in an orderly way.

> **PRINCIPLES OF PARLIAMENTARY PROCEDURE**
> 1. Issues are debated and voted on one at a time.
> 2. The decision of the majority rules.
> 3. Those in the minority are allowed to present their views.
> 4. Every member has the right to vote or not to vote.
> 5. Open discussion of every issue is assured.

EXERCISE A: Understanding Parliamentary Procedure. Answer the questions below.

1. Why is it important to use parliamentary procedure to hold a discussion involving more than ten people? _____

2. If one issue has been discussed but not voted on, can another issue be discussed? Explain. _____

3. What does a simple majority consist of? _____

4. How are minority rights protected? _____

5. Does every member have to speak at each meeting? Explain. _____

EXERCISE B: More Work with Parliamentary Procedure. Answer the questions below.

1. Why is open discussion of every issue assured? _____

2. What is a *quorum*? _____

3. What are the eight steps involved in conducting a meeting? _____

4. What is a motion? _____

5. List four of the steps involved in carrying out a motion. _____

Copyright © by Prentice-Hall, Inc.

NAME _____ CLASS _____ DATE _____

33.3 Public Speaking

Recognizing Different Kinds of Speeches

Choose the kind of speech you will give by considering both the purpose of the speech and your audience.

KINDS OF SPEECHES	
Expository	Uses facts to explain an idea, a process, or an object
Persuasive	Uses opinions supported by facts to persuade an audience to agree with the speaker's position or to take some action
Entertaining	Offers the audience something to enjoy
Extemporaneous	Requires the speaker to rely on knowledge and speaking skills to speak without a formally prepared manuscript

Giving a Speech

Follow a series of steps to plan, prepare, and deliver your speech.

DELIVERING A SPEECH
1. Establish eye contact with several people in the audience.
2. Briefly look over your note cards before you start speaking.
3. Refer to your note cards as seldom as possible while speaking.

Evaluating a Speech

Evaluate a speech in a way that offers benefits to the speaker and to yourself.

EXERCISE A: Planning a Speech. Complete the activities below.

1. Choose the kind of speech you will give. _____
2. Choose an appropriate topic. _____
3. Gather the information you need to give your speech, taking notes on separate paper.
4. On a separate sheet of paper, write an outline that presents the information you gathered in #3 in a logical manner.
5. Prepare note cards that you can use when you deliver your speech.

EXERCISE B: Evaluating a Speech. Evaluate a speech given in class by answering the questions below.

1. What type of speech was given? _____
2. Did the speaker introduce the topic clearly and develop it well? Support your answer. _____
3. Did the speaker support main ideas with appropriate details? Give two examples. _____
4. Did the speaker's movements confirm or contradict his or her words? Where? How? _____
5. Did the speaker vary the rate of his or her speaking? _____

NAME _____ CLASS _____ DATE _____

33.4 Public Debate

The Nature of Debate

A debate is a formal public discussion in which opposing sides use reasoned arguments to arrive at a decision that declares one side the winner.

THE TWO SIDES OF A DEBATE	
Affirmative	Upholds the proposition (a positive statement of the issue under debate) by demanding that the present situation be changed
Negative	Presents arguments to disprove attacks made on the present situation by the affirmative

Preparing to Debate

Prepare to debate by analyzing the proposition, preparing sound evidence and reasoning, and working with your partner to build the case.

Holding a Debate

In a debate each team must present a strong case and refute the opposition's arguments as well.

EXERCISE A: Understanding the Nature of Debate. Answer the questions below.

1. How does a debate differ from other kinds of group discussions? _____
_____
2. What is the purpose of a debate? _____
_____
3. What is a proposition? _____
4. What is the responsibility of proving that the proposition is true called? _____
5. Write an appropriate debate proposition. _____
_____

EXERCISE B: Preparing to Debate. Examine the proposition below. Then complete the work that follows.

   PROPOSITION: Resolved, cigarette smoking in public places should be restricted.

1. Which side are you going to take? _____
2. Are there any problems being created by the present situation? Support your answer. ____
_____
3. What other approach, if any, is available to solve the problem? _____
_____
4. Gather evidence to support your position. _____
_____
_____
_____
_____
_____
_____
5. On a separate piece of paper, organize the evidence you gathered in #4 into a modified outline.

Copyright © by Prentice-Hall, Inc.

NAME _____ CLASS _____ DATE _____

33.5 Listening Skills

Improving Your Listening Skills

Learn to take mental and written notes on main ideas and major details as you listen.

LISTENING FOR MAIN IDEAS
1. Listen carefully to the beginning statements of the speaker.
2. Visualize the main ideas and restate them in your own words.
3. Decide whether the speaker's examples, facts, and statistics support the main ideas you have in mind.

Listening Critically

Listen critically in order to interpret and evaluate a speaker's words.

TECHNIQUES FOR CRITICAL LISTENING	
Fact and Opinion	Speakers may give opinions without supporting them with pertinent facts.
Denotation and Connotation	Speakers may choose words with unfavorable connotations to present someone or something unfavorably.
Euphemisms	Speakers can use euphemisms to soften the meaning that more direct words would convey.
Self-important Language	Speakers sometimes use self-important language to try to impress listeners.

EXERCISE A: Listening for Important Information. Write down the main idea and major details of a lecture given in one of your classes in the spaces provided below.

1. Main idea _____
2. Major detail _____
3. Major detail _____
4. Major detail _____
5. Major detail _____

EXERCISE B: Developing Critical Listening Skills. Listen critically to a political speech on radio or television. Then complete the activities below.

1. What was the topic of the speech? _____
2. Did the speaker support all of his or her opinions with facts? Support your answer. _____

3. Did the speaker at any time choose words with unfavorable connotations to present someone or something unfavorably? If so, give an example. _____

4. Did the speaker use euphemisms? If so, give an example. _____

5. Did the speaker use self-important language? If so, give an example. _____